180 Days of

SCIENCE

for Sixth Grade

Authors
Bebra Bayne and Lauren Homayoun

SHELL EDUCATION

Earth & Space
Life
Physical

Publishing Credits

Corinne Burton, M.A.Ed., *Publisher*
Conni Medina, M.A.Ed., *Managing Editor*
Emily R. Smith, M.A.Ed., *Content Director*
Shaun Bernadou, *Art Director*
Lynette Ordoñez, *Editor*

Image Credits

p. 96 testing/Shutterstock.com;
p. 181 Paolo Bona/Shutterstock.com;
all other images from iStock and/or Shutterstock.

Standards

© 2014 Mid-continent Research for Education and Learning (McREL)
NGSS Lead States. 2013. Next Generation Science Standards: For States, By States.
Washington, DC: The National Academies Press.

For information on how this resource meets national and other state standards, see pages 10–13. You may also review this information by visiting our website at www.teachercreatedmaterials.com/administrators/correlations/ and following the on-screen directions.

Shell Education

A division of Teacher Created Materials
5301 Oceanus Drive
Huntington Beach, CA 92649-1030
www.tcmpub.com/shell-education

ISBN 978-1-4258-1412-0
©2018 Shell Educational Publishing, Inc.

51412—180 Days of Science

© *Shell Education*

Table of Contents

Introduction 3

How to Use This Book 4

Standards Correlations 9

Daily Practice Pages 14

Answer Key 194

Teacher Resources 204

Digital Resources 216

Introduction

With today's science and technology, there are more resources than ever to help students understand how the world works. Information about science experiments you can do at home is widely available online. Many students have experience with physics concepts from games.

While students may be familiar with many of the topics discussed in this book, it is not uncommon for them to have misconceptions about certain subjects. It is important for students to learn how to apply scientific practices in a classroom setting and within their lives.

Science is the study of the physical and natural world through observation and experiment. Not only is it important for students to learn scientific facts, but it is important for them to develop a thirst for knowledge. This leads to students who are anxious to learn and who understand how to follow practices that will lead them to the answers they seek.

The Need for Practice

To be successful in science, students must understand how people interact with the physical world. They must not only master scientific practices but also learn how to look at the world with curiosity. Through repeated practice, students will learn how a variety of factors affect the world in which they live.

Understanding Assessment

In addition to providing opportunities for frequent practice, teachers must be able to assess students' scientific understandings. This allows teachers to adequately address students' misconceptions, build on their current understandings, and challenge them appropriately. Assessment is a long-term process that involves careful analysis of student responses from discussions, projects, or practice sheets. The data gathered from assessments should be used to inform instruction: slow down, speed up, or reteach. This type of assessment is called *formative assessment*.

How to Use This Book

Weekly Structure

All 36 weeks of this book follow a regular weekly structure. The book is divided into three sections: Life Science, Physical Science, and Earth and Space Science. The book is structured to give students a strong foundation on which to build throughout the year. It is also designed to adequately prepare them for state standardized tests.

Each week focuses on one topic. Day 1 sets the stage by providing background information on the topic that students will need throughout the week. In Day 2, students analyze data related to the topic. Day 3 leads students through developing scientific questions. Day 4 guides students through planning a solution. Finally, Day 5 helps students communicate results from observations or investigations.

 Day 1—Learning Content: Students will read grade-appropriate content and answer questions about it.

 Day 2—Analyzing Data: Students will analyze scientific data and answer questions about it.

 Day 3—Developing Questions: Students will read a scenario related to the topic, answer questions, and formulate a scientific question about the information.

 Day 4—Planning Solutions: Students will read a scenario related to the topic, answer questions, and develop a solution or plan an investigation.

 Day 5—Communicating Results: Students accurately communicate the results of an investigation or demonstrate what they learned throughout the week.

Three Strands of Science

This book allows students to explore the three strands of science: life science, physical science, and earth and space science. Life science teaches students about the amazing living things on our planet and how they interact in ecosystems. Physical science introduces students to physics and chemistry concepts that will lay the groundwork for deeper understanding later in their education. Earth and space science familiarizes students with the wonders of the cosmos and the relationships between the sun, Earth, moon, and stars.

How to Use This Book *(cont.)*

Weekly Topics

The following chart shows the weekly focus topics that are covered during each week of instruction.

Unit	Week	Science Topic
Life Science	1	What are Living Things Made of?
	2	The Function of Cells
	3	The Role of Photosynthesis
	4	What Happens to Food After it is Consumed?
	5	Resources and Population
	6	Structure, Behavior, and Survival
	7	What Affects a Plant's Growth
	8	What Can Fossils Tell Us?
	9	Seeing Change Over Time in Fossils
	10	Unity in Organisms
	11	Genetics & Survival
	12	Population Levels
Physical Science	1	Models of Molecules
	2	Properties Before and After Reactions
	3	Synthetics from Natural Materials
	4	Mass Conservation in Chemical Reactions
	5	Car Crashes
	6	Balanced and Unbalanced Forces
	7	Is Earth a Magnet?
	8	Kinetic Energy
	9	Static Electricity
	10	Making a Solar Cooker
	11	Sound Waves and Energy
	12	Light Waves and Absorption
Earth and Space Science	1	Phases, Eclipses, and Seasons
	2	Gravity in the Solar System
	3	Objects in the Solar System
	4	Learning Earth's History
	5	Changes in Earth's Surfaces
	6	Plate Motions and Earth's History
	7	Cycles of Matter and Energy on Earth
	8	Effects of Weathering and Erosion of Natural Resources
	9	Ocean Temperatures and Weather Patterns
	10	Charting Human Activities and Climate Change
	11	Taking Care of Our Environment
	12	Population and Resource Conservation

How to Use This Book *(cont.)*

Best Practices for This Series

- Use the practice pages to introduce important science topics to your students.

- Use the Weekly Topics chart on page 5 to align the content to what you're covering in class. Then, treat the pages in this book as jumping off points for that content.

- Use the practice pages as formative assessment of the science strands and key topics.

- Use the weekly themes to engage students in content that is new to them.

- Encourage students to independently learn more about the topics introduced in this series.

- Lead teacher-directed discussions of the vocabulary and concepts presented in some of the more complex weeks.

- Support students in practicing the varied types of questions asked throughout the practice pages.

- When possible, have students participate in hands-on activities to answer the questions they generate and do the investigations they plan.

Using the Resources

An answer key for all days can be found on pages 194–203. Rubrics for Day 3 (developing questions), Day 4 (planning solutions), and Day 5 (communicating results) can be found on pages 210–212 and in the Digital Resources. Use the answer keys and rubrics to assess students' work. Be sure to share these rubrics with students so that they know what is expected of them.

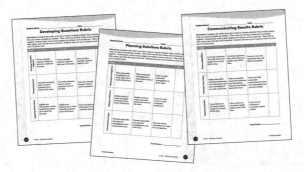

How to Use This Book (cont.)

Diagnostic Assessment

Teachers can use the practice pages as diagnostic assessments. The data analysis tools included with the book enable teachers or parents to quickly score students' work and monitor their progress. Teachers and parents can see which skills students may need to target further to develop proficiency.

Students will learn science content, how to analyze data, how to develop scientific questions, how to plan solutions, and how to accurately communicate results. You can assess students' learning using the answer key for all days. Rubrics are also provided on pages 210–212 for Days 3–5 to help you further assess key analytical skills that are needed for success with the scientific practices. Then, record their scores on the Practice Page Item Analysis sheets (pages 213–215). These charts are provided as PDFs, Microsoft Word® files, and Microsoft Excel® files. Teachers can input data into the electronic files directly, or they can print the pages.

To Complete the Practice Page Analysis Charts

- Write or type students' names in the far-left column. Depending on the number of students, more than one copy of the form may be needed or you may need to add rows.

  - The science strands are indicated across the tops of the charts.

  - Students should be assessed every four weeks, as indicated in the first rows of the charts.

- For each student, evaluate his or her work over the past four weeks using the answer key for Days 1 and 2 and the rubrics for Days 3–5.

- Review students' work for the weeks indicated in the chart. For example, if using the *Life Science Analysis Chart* for the first time, review students' work from weeks 1–4. Add the scores for Days 1 and 2 for each student, and record those in the appropriate columns. Then, write students' rubric scores for Days 3–5 in the corresponding columns. Use these scores as benchmarks to determine how each student is performing.

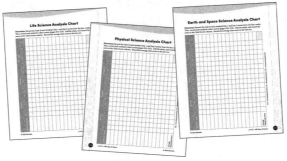

Digital Resources

The Digital Resources contain digital copies of the rubrics, analysis sheets, and standards correlations. See page 216 for more information.

How to Use This Book *(cont.)*

Using the Results to Differentiate Instruction

Once results are gathered and analyzed, teachers can use the results to inform the way they differentiate instruction. The data can help determine which science skills and topics are the most difficult for students and which students need additional instructional support and continued practice.

Whole-Class Support

The results of the diagnostic analysis may show that the entire class is struggling with certain science topics. If these concepts have been taught in the past, this indicates that further instruction or reteaching is necessary. If these concepts have not been taught in the past, this data is a great preassessment and may demonstrate that students do not have a working knowledge of the concepts. Thus, careful planning for the length of the unit(s) or lesson(s) must be considered, and additional front-loading may be required.

Small-Group or Individual Support

The results of the diagnostic analysis may show that an individual student or a small group of students is struggling with certain science skills. If these concepts have been taught in the past, this indicates that further instruction or reteaching is necessary. Consider pulling these students aside to instruct them further on the concepts while others are working independently. Students may also benefit from extra practice using games or computer-based resources.

Teachers can also use the results to help identify proficient individual students or groups of students who are ready for enrichment or above-grade-level instruction. These students may benefit from independent learning contracts or more challenging activities.

Standards Correlations

Shell Education is committed to producing educational materials that are research and standards based. In this effort, we have correlated all of our products to the academic standards of all 50 states, the District of Columbia, the Department of Defense Dependents Schools, and all Canadian provinces.

How to Find Standards Correlations

To print a customized correlation report of this product for your state, visit our website at **www.teachercreatedmaterials.com/administrators/correlations/** and follow the on-screen directions. If you require assistance in printing correlation reports, please contact our Customer Service Department at 1-877-777-3450.

Purpose and Intent of Standards

The Every Student Succeeds Act (ESSA) mandates that all states adopt challenging academic standards that help students meet the goal of college and career readiness. While many states already adopted academic standards prior to ESSA, the act continues to hold states accountable for detailed and comprehensive standards.

Standards are designed to focus instruction and guide adoption of curricula. Standards are statements that describe the criteria necessary for students to meet specific academic goals. They define the knowledge, skills, and content students should acquire at each level. Standards are also used to develop standardized tests to evaluate students' academic progress. Teachers are required to demonstrate how their lessons meet state standards. State standards are used in the development of all of our products, so educators can be assured they meet the academic requirements of each state.

McREL Compendium

Each year, McREL analyzes state standards and revises the compendium to produce a general compilation of national standards. The standards listed on pages 10–11 support the objectives presented throughout the weeks.

Next Generation Science Standards

This set of national standards aims to incorporate knowledge and process standards into a cohesive framework. The standards listed on pages 11–13 support the objectives presented throughout the weeks.

Standards Correlations *(cont.)*

180 Days of Science is designed to give students daily practice in the three strands of science. The weeks support the McREL standards and NGSS performance expectations listed in the charts below.

McREL Standards		
Standard	Weeks	Unit
Knows that all organisms are composed of cells, which are the fundamental units of life; most organisms are single cells, but other organisms are multicellular.	1	Life Science
Knows that cells convert energy obtained from food to carry on the many functions needed to sustain life.	2	Life Science
Knows how energy is transferred through food webs in an ecosystem.	3	Life Science
Knows factors that affect the number and types of organisms an ecosystem can support.	5	Life Science
Knows basic ideas related to biological evolution.	6, 11, 12	Life Science
Knows that the characteristics of an organism can be described in terms of a combination of traits; some traits are inherited through the coding of genetic material, and others result from environmental factors.	7	Life Science
Knows that the fossil record, through geologic evidence, documents the appearance, diversification, and extinction of many life forms.	8	Life Science
Knows evidence that supports the idea that there is unity among organisms despite the fact that some species look very different.	9, 10	Life Science
Knows that matter is made up of tiny particles called atoms, and different arrangements of atoms into groups compose all substances.	1	Physical Science
Knows that substances react chemically in characteristic ways with other substances to form new substances with different characteristic properties.	2	Physical Science
Understands the conservation of mass in physical and chemical change.	4	Physical Science
Understands the effects of balanced and unbalanced forces on an object's motion.	6	Physical Science
Knows that heat energy flows from warmer materials or regions to cooler ones through conduction, convection, and radiation.	10	Physical Science
Knows that waves have energy and interact with matter and can transfer energy.	11, 12	Physical Science
Knows how the tilt of the Earth's axis and the Earth's revolution around the Sun affects seasons and weather patterns.	1	Earth and Space Science
Knows how the regular and predictable motions of the Earth and Moon explain phenomena on Earth.	1	Earth and Space Science
Knows that gravitational force keeps planets in orbit around the Sun and moons in orbit around the planets.	2	Earth and Space Science
Knows characteristics and movement patterns of the planets in our solar system.	3	Earth and Space Science
Knows how successive layers of sedimentary rock and the fossils contained within them can be used to confirm the age, history, and changing life forms of the Earth, and how this evidence is affected by the folding, breaking, and uplifting of layers.	4	Earth and Space Science

Standards Correlations *(cont.)*

McREL Standards		
Standard	**Weeks**	**Unit**
Knows that fossils provide important evidence of how environmental conditions have changed on the Earth over time.	6	Earth and Space Science
Knows the composition and structure of the Earth's atmosphere.	9	Earth and Space Science

Next Generation Science Standards					
Unit	**Week**	**Performance Expectation**	**Science and Engineering Practices**	**Disciplinary Core Ideas**	**Cross-Cutting Concepts**
Life Science	1	Conduct an investigation to provide evidence that living things are made of cells; either one cell or many different numbers and types of cells.	Planning and Carrying Out Investigations	Structure and Function	Scale, Proportion, and Quantity
	2	Develop and use a model to describe the function of a cell as a whole, and ways that parts of cells contribute to the function.	Developing and Using Models	Structure and Function	Structure and Function
	3	Construct a scientific explanation based on evidence for the role of photosynthesis in the cycling of matter and flow of energy into and out of organisms.	Constructing Explanations and Designing Solutions	Organization for Matter and Energy Flow in Organisms	Energy and Matter
	4	Develop a model to describe how food is rearranged through chemical reactions, forming new molecules that support growth and/or release energy as this matter moves through an organism.	Developing and Using Models	Organization for Matter and Energy Flow in Organisms	Energy and Matter
	5	Analyze and interpret data to provide evidence for the effects of resource availability on organisms and populations of organisms in an ecosystem.	Analyzing and Interpreting Data	Interdependent Relationships in Ecosystems	Cause and Effect
	6	Use argument-based or empirical evidence and scientific reasoning to support an explanation for how characteristic animal behaviors and specialized plant structures affect the probability of successful reproduction of animals and plants, respectively.	Engaging in Argument from Evidence	Growth and Development of Organisms	Cause and Effect
	7	Construct a scientific explanation based on evidence for how environmental and genetic factors influence the growth of organisms.	Constructing Explanations and Designing Solutions	Growth and Development of Organisms	Cause and Effect
	8	Analyze and interpret data for patterns in the fossil record that document the existence, diversity, extinction, and change of life forms throughout the history of life on Earth, under the assumption that natural laws operate today as in the past.	Analyzing and Interpreting Data	Evidence of Common Ancestry and Diversity	Patterns
	9	Apply scientific ideas to construct an explanation for the anatomical similarities and differences among modern organisms and between modern and fossil organisms to infer evolutionary relationships.	Constructing Explanations and Designing Solutions	Evidence of Common Ancestry and Diversity	Patterns
	10	Analyze displays of pictorial data to compare patterns of similarities in the embryological development across multiple species to identify relationships not evident in the fully-formed anatomy.	Analyzing and Interpreting Data	Evidence of Common Ancestry and Diversity	Patterns

Standards Correlations *(cont.)*

Unit	Week	Performance Expectation	Science and Engineering Practices	Disciplinary Core Ideas	Cross-Cutting Concepts
		Next Generation Science Standards			
Life Science	11	Construct an explanation based on evidence that describes how genetic variations of traits in a population increase some individuals' probability of surviving and reproducing in a specific environment.	Constructing Explanations and Designing Solutions	Natural Selection	Cause and Effect
	12	Use mathematical representations to support explanations of how natural selection may lead to increases and decreases of specific traits in populations over time.	Using Mathematics and Computational Thinking	Adaptation	Cause and Effect
Physical Science	1	Develop models to describe the atomic composition of simple molecules and extended structures.	Developing and Using Models	Structure and Properties of Matter	Scale, Proportion, and Quantity
	2	Analyze and interpret data on the properties of substances before and after the substances interact, to determine if a chemical reaction has occurred.	Analyzing and Interpreting Data	Chemical Reactions	Patterns
	3	Gather and make sense of information to describe that synthetic materials come from natural resources, and impact society.	Developing and Using Models	Chemical Reactions	Structure and Function
	4	Develop and use a model to describe how the total number of atoms does not change in a chemical reaction, and thus mass is conserved.	Developing and Using Models	Chemical Reactions	Energy and Matter
	5	Apply Newton's Third Law to design a solution to a problem involving the motion of two colliding objects.	Constructing Explanations and Designing Solutions	Forces and Motion	Systems and System Models
	6	Plan an investigation to provide evidence that the change in an object's motion depends on the sum of the forces on the object and the mass of the object.	Planning and Carrying Out Investigations	Forces and Motion	Stability and Change
	7	Ask questions about data to determine the factors that affect the strength of electric and magnetic forces.	Asking Questions and Defining Problems	Types of Interactions	Cause and Effect
	8	Construct and interpret graphical displays of data to describe the relationships of kinetic energy to the mass of an object and to the speed of an object.	Analyzing & Interpreting Data	Definitions of Energy	Scale, Proportion, and Quantity
	9	Develop a model to describe that when the arrangement of objects interacting at a distance changes, different amounts of potential energy are stored in the system.	Analyzing & Interpreting Data	Definitions of Energy	Systems and System Models
	10	Apply scientific principles to design, construct, and test a device that either minimizes or maximizes thermal energy transfer.	Constructing Explanations and Designing Solutions	Definitions of Energy	Energy and Matter
	11	Use mathematical representations to describe a simple model for waves that includes how the amplitude of a wave is related to the energy in a wave.	Using Mathematics and Computational Thinking	Wave Properties	Patterns
	12	Develop and use a model to describe that waves are reflected, absorbed, or transmitted through various materials.	Developing and Using Models	Wave Properties Electromagnetic Radiation	Structure and Function

Standards Correlations *(cont.)*

Unit	Week	Performance Expectation	Next Generation Science Standards		
			Science and Engineering Practices	Disciplinary Core Ideas	Cross-Cutting Concepts
Earth and Space Science	1	Develop and use a model of the Earth-Sun-Moon system to describe the cyclic patterns of lunar phases, eclipses of the Sun and Moon, and seasons.	Developing and Using Models	The Universe and Its Stars	Patterns
	2	Develop and use a model to describe the role of gravity in the motions within galaxies and the solar system.	Developing and Using Models	Earth and the Solar System	Systems and System Models
	3	Analyze and interpret data to determine scale properties of objects in the solar system.	Analyzing & Interpreting Data	Earth and the Solar System	Scale, Proportion, and Quantity
	4	Construct a scientific explanation based on evidence from rock strata for how the geologic time scale is used to organize Earth's 4.6 billion-year-old history.	Constructing Explanations and Designing Solutions	The History of Planet Earth	Scale, Proportion, and Quantity
	5	Construct an explanation based on evidence for how geoscience processes have changed Earth's surface at varying times and spatial scales.	Constructing Explanations and Designing Solutions	Earth's Materials & Systems	Scale Proportion and Quantity
	6	Analyze and interpret data on the distribution of fossils and rocks, continental shapes, and sea-floor structures to provide evidence of the past plate motions.	Analyzing and Interpreting Data Scientific Knowledge is Open to Revision in Light of New Evidence	The History of Planet Earth Plate Tectonics and Large-Scale Interactions	Patterns
	7	Develop a model to describe the cycling of Earth's materials and the flow of energy that drives this process.	Developing and Using Models	Earth's Materials and Systems	Stability and Change
	8	Construct a scientific explanation based on evidence for how the uneven distributions of Earth's mineral, energy, and groundwater resources are the result of past and current geoscience processes.	Constructing Explanations and Designing Solutions	Natural Resources	Cause and Effect
	9	Collect data to provide evidence for how the motions and complex interactions of air masses result in changes in weather conditions.	Planning and Carrying Out Investigations	The Role of Water in Earth's Surface Processes	Cause and Effect
	10	Ask questions to clarify evidence of the factors that have caused the rise in global temperatures over the past century.	Asking Questions and Defining Problems	Global Climate Change	Stability and Change
	11	Apply scientific principles to design a method for monitoring and minimizing a human impact on the environment.	Constructing Explanations and Designing Solutions	Human Impacts on Earth Systems	Cause and Effect
	12	Construct an argument supported by evidence for how increases in human population and per capita consumption of natural resources impact Earth's systems.	Engaging in Argument from Evidence	Human Impacts on Earth Systems	Cause and Effect

Learning Content

Name: Dex

Date: _____

Directions: Read the text, and answer the questions.

What Is a Cell?

A cell is the smallest unit of life that can reproduce itself independently. All living things are made of cells. An organism with only one cell is unicellular. An organism with many cells is multicellular. Your body is multicellular, composed of trillions of cells.

Each cell is filled with a gel-like material called *cytoplasm*. It includes the nucleus, a structure that contains DNA—the genetic code for all life. Inside the nucleus is the *nucleolus* that produces ribosomes—molecules that make proteins. Another important part of the cell is the mitochondria, where food and oxygen combine to create usable energy. A protective barrier called the cell membrane surrounds each cell, controlling what enters (food) and leaves (waste). A plant cell has a *cell wall* on its outermost part, covering the cell membrane. An animal cell does not have a cell wall.

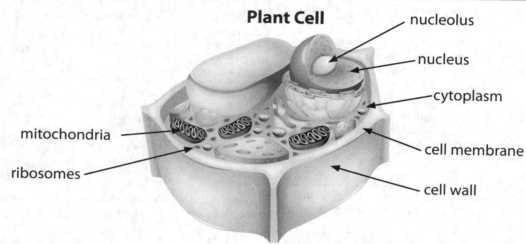

Plant Cell

nucleolus

nucleus

cytoplasm

mitochondria

cell membrane

ribosomes

cell wall

1. Which structure is found only in plant cells?

a. cell wall

b. nucleus

c. cytoplasm

d. ribosome

2. Which part of a cell contains the genetic code for all life?

a. cytoplasm

b. nucleus

c. mitochondria

d. cell wall

3. Why do you think cells are called "the building blocks of life"?

Because they shape you

Name: _Desi_ **Date:** _8-18-22_

Directions: Study the diagrams, and answer the questions.

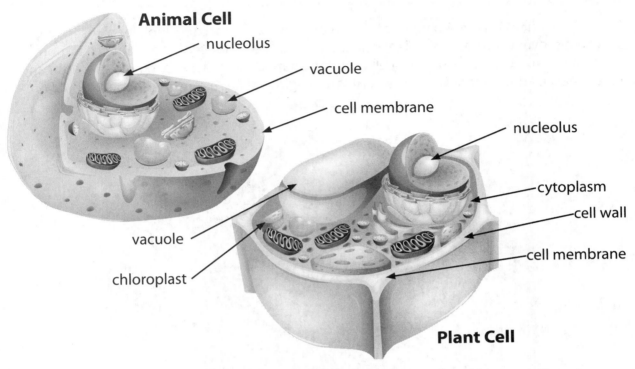

Animal Cell
nucleolus
vacuole
cell membrane
nucleolus
cytoplasm
cell wall
vacuole
cell membrane
chloroplast
Plant Cell

1. What is the oval structure in both plant and animal cells that looks like an egg?

    a. ribosomes

    b. nucleolus

    c. mitochondria

    d. cell membrane

2. What encloses the cell?

    a. nucleus

    b. chloroplast

    c. cell membrane

    d. vacuole

3. List some differences you see between the plant and animal cells in the pictures.

    cell wall, choroplast

Developing Questions

Name: Dex

Date:

Directions: Read the text, and answer the questions.

In science class, when you observe a cell under a microscope, look for clues to help you discover whether it is a plant cell or an animal cell. Notice that a plant cell is more rigid in structure because of its cell wall. It is shaped more like a rectangle. Because an animal cell does not have a cell wall, it is less rigid and has a rounder shape.

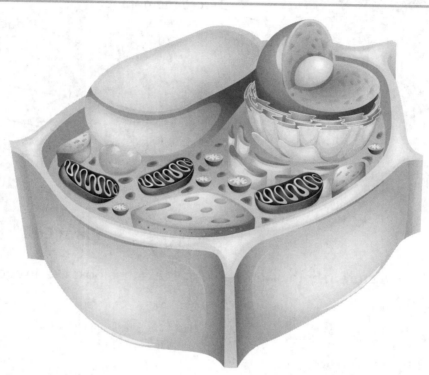

1. What does the wall at the edges of the cell tell you?

   a. It is a plant cell.

   b. It is an animal cell.

   c. The cell is strong.

   d. The cell is waterproof.

2. What does the nucleus of the cell hold?

   a. It holds water.

   b. It holds DNA information.

   c. It holds the cell wall.

   d. It holds the cell membrane.

3. Based on what you have learned about cells, write a question.

   What does a plant cell look like

Name: Dex

Date: _____

Directions: Read the text, and answer the questions.

> While using a microscope to look at a slide, you determine that what you see under the microscope is a plant cell. Your teacher asks you to explain why you think it is a plant cell, and not an animal cell. How can you convince your teacher this is a plant cell?

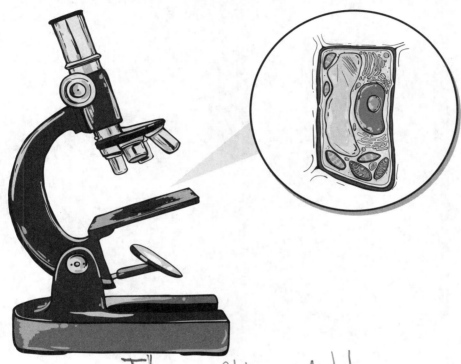

1. You can show your teacher ___The cell.wall___

    (a.) the cell wall   **b.** the cell membrane

    c. the nucleolus   **d.** the cytoplasm

2. You can also point out the general shape of the cell, which is ___rectangular___

    a. large   (b.) rectangular

    c. thin   **d.** round

3. How are animal cells and plant cells shaped differently?

___The animal cell is round___
___and the plant is rigid___

Communicating Results

Name: Dex **Date:** _____

Directions: Study the diagram, and answer the questions.

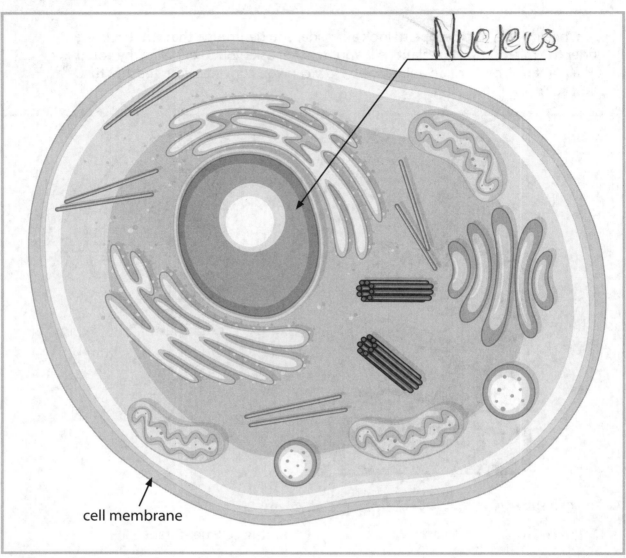

Nucleus

cell membrane

1. On the diagram, write the word "nucleus" on the line that is pointing to the nucleus.

2. Does the diagram represent a plant cell or an animal cell?

Animal cell

3. How do you know?

Because it doesnt have a rigid structure and it has no choroPlast

Name: Dex

Date: _____

Directions: Read the text, and answer the questions.

Organelles Within the Cells

The interior of a cell is organized into compartments called *organelles*. Plant cells and animal cells have many of the same kinds of organelles. They also have organelles that are different. Plants have organelles called chloroplasts that animal cells do not have. Chloroplasts contain a pigment called chlorophyll. It captures the sun's energy to transform water and carbon dioxide into sugar, to feed the plant. This process is called photosynthesis.

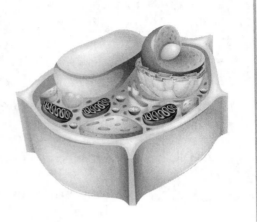

1. Organelles called chloroplasts provide food for the plant by using the sun's energy. What is this process called?

   a. mitochondria

   b. mutation

   c. photosynthesis

   d. glucose

2. The cells of plants and animals _____.

   a. have all identical organelles

   b. have all different organelles

   c. have some of the same organelles, and some organelles that are different

   d. have organelles that change the organism from plant to animal

3. Why do you think animals do not need chloroplasts and chlorophyll in their cells?

   Because they have mouths
   to get food into them
   to survive.

Analyzing Data

Name: _____ Date: _____

Directions: Study the chart of cellular functions, and answer the questions.

What Do Cells Do?			
Cell Part	**Function**	**Present in Animal Cells**	**Present in Plant Cells**
nucleus	controls all activities, contains genetic material	X	X
nucleolus	in nucleus; makes ribosomes	X	X
cell membrane	allows substances to pass in and out of the cell	X	X
cell wall	tough barrier that supports the cell		X
mitochondria	energy center	X	X
chloroplasts	contain chlorophyll needed for photosynthesis		X
ribosomes	makes proteins	X	X
vacuole	stores food, nutrients, and sap (salts and sugars)	X	X

1. What structures are found only in plant cells?

   a. ribosomes and cell walls

   b. mitochrondria and cell walls

   c. cell walls and chloroplasts

   d. nucleus and chloroplasts

2. What part provides energy for the cell?

   a. mitochondria

   b. ribosomes

   c. chloroplasts

   d. nucleus

3. How are plant and animal cells similar?

   _____

   _____

Name: _____ **Date:** _____

Directions: Read the text, and answer the questions.

Water is essential for plants to live. If you place a white carnation into a glass of water, and then add blue food coloring to the water, the white carnation will begin to turn blue, through the process of *osmosis*. When water molecules distribute themselves evenly within a space (such as a stem, and flowers and leaves) this is called osmosis. It is the way that all parts of a plant receive water.

1. Without osmosis, what do you think might happen to a plant's leaves and flowers and stems?

    a. They might like having no water.

    b. They might die.

    c. They might grow.

    d. none of the above

2. What is a good definition of osmosis?

    a. The movement of water to evenly distribute itself.

    b. The leakage of water into plant parts and other living things.

    c. It is similar to photosynthesis.

    d. It is the process of a flower changing color.

3. Write a question about the process of osmosis, based on what you have learned.

    _____

    _____

    _____

    _____

Developing Questions

Planning Solutions

Name: _____ **Date:** _____

Directions: Read the text, and answer the questions.

After your experiment with the white carnation, you want to see if other types of flowers can absorb color through osmosis. You have a red geranium, a white rose, a yellow daisy, and a purple iris. You want to see if you can turn any of them blue.

1. What could you do to control the results of the experiment?

   a. Put each flower in a separate vase with water only, for 24 hours, before you add food coloring, to see what happens (as a control).

   b. Add the same amount of blue food coloring to all vases, at the same time.

   c. Write in your lab journal exactly what you did and the results you saw.

   d. all of the above

2. How would you test celery if you wanted to see the results of osmosis?

   a. Use four stalks of celery instead of four flowers, and do exactly what you did with the carnations.

   b. Change the food coloring to another color.

   c. Keep the celery in the water for twice as long as you kept the carnations in water.

   d. Use four stalks of celery in water with no food coloring.

3. What do you think might happen if you put a freshly cut stalk of celery in a glass of water with red food coloring for 24 hours?

   _____

   _____

   _____

Name: _____ **Date:** _____

Directions: Read the text, and study the data. Title the graph, and create a graph that shows the length of time it took for each color to be absorbed. Then, answer the questions.

Assume that you did the carnation experiment with five different food colorings. You have tested to see which food coloring is absorbed into the carnations most quickly. Your results are shown to the right.

Red: 12 hours

Yellow: 24 hours

Green: 6 hours

Blue: 3 hours

Purple: 9 hours

Communicating Results

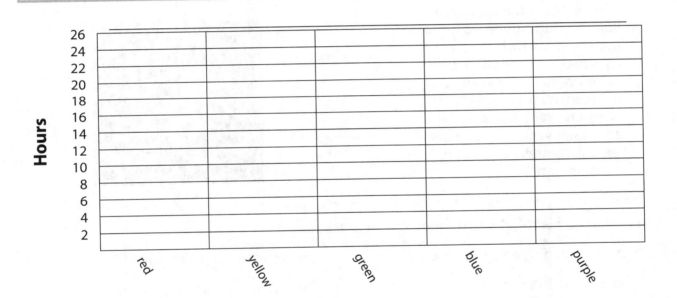

1. Which color was absorbed most quickly?

   _____

2. Which color was absorbed most slowly?

   _____

3. Which color took 9 hours to absorb?

   _____

Name: _____ **Date:** _____

Directions: Read the text, and answer the questions.

Photosynthesis

Plants make the food they need through a process called photosynthesis. The process begins when the chlorophyll inside a plant's cells absorbs light energy, usually from the sun. At the same time, carbon dioxide enters the plant through its leaves, and its roots absorb water from the soil. The water, carbon dioxide, and light combine in the leaves to make sugar, which the plant uses to grow. Any sugar the plant doesn't need right away is stored as starch in the roots. Then the plants release oxygen and water vapor through their leaves. This release is called transpiration.

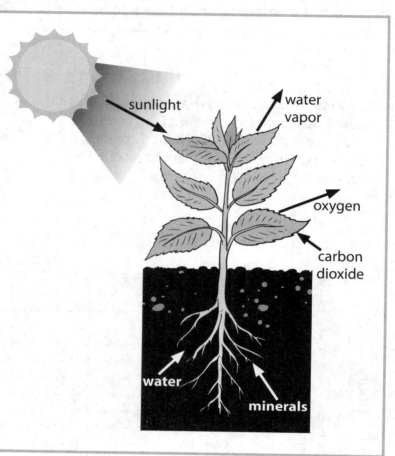

1. What do plants release through their leaves?

   a. carbon dioxide and oxygen

   c. sugar and water

   b. oxygen and water vapor

   d. carbon dioxide and sugar

2. What happens during photosynthesis?

   a. Plants stop growing.

   c. Plants create the food they need.

   b. Plants store sugar in their roots.

   d. both b and c

3. What happens during transpiration?

   _____

   _____

   _____

51412—180 Days of Science

Learning Content

Name: _____ Date: _____

Directions: Study the diagram, and answer the questions.

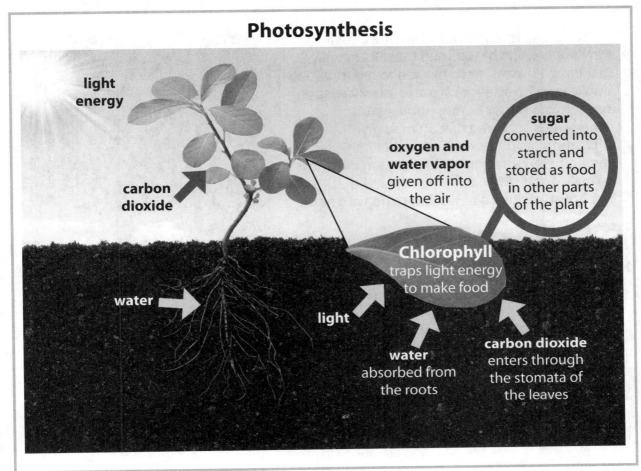

Photosynthesis

light energy

carbon dioxide

water

oxygen and water vapor given off into the air

sugar converted into starch and stored as food in other parts of the plant

Chlorophyll traps light energy to make food

light

water absorbed from the roots

carbon dioxide enters through the stomata of the leaves

1. What do plants need to create energy?

a. light, carbon dioxide, and water

b. carbon dioxide and oxygen

c. water and sugar

d. sugar and oxygen

2. Chlorophyll traps light energy to make _____.

a. dirt

b. metal

c. food

d. iron

3. When plants give off oxygen, where does it go?

_____

_____

Developing Questions

Name: _____ **Date:** _____

Directions: Read the text, and answer the questions.

Kara is learning how to take care of her new puppy. She has learned that all animals, including humans, need oxygen to breathe. She also learned in science class that plants release oxygen into the air during photosynthesis. When she discovered that animals give off carbon dioxide when they exhale, she remembered that plants need carbon dioxide to make food. After that, she decided that her house needed a new plant to go with her new puppy.

1. What would happen if all the plants on Earth died?

   a. oxygen and carbon dioxide would mix

   b. the carbon dioxide level would increase

   c. the oxygen level would decrease

   d. both b and c

2. What do plants release into the air during photosynthesis?

   a. carbon dioxide

   b. calories

   c. oxygen

   d. sugar

3. What questions could Kara ask about plant placement in her house?

   _____

   _____

   _____

   _____

Planning Solutions

Name: _____   **Date:** _____

Directions: Read the text, and answer the questions.

Plants absorb carbon dioxide, and they can also absorb other substances. Scientists have studied the effect that living plants inside buildings can have on the quality of indoor air. They have discovered that having indoor plants makes the air much cleaner because the plants trap pollutants.

1. Your bedroom smells stale. You want to be environmentally safe. What can you do to improve the quality of the air?

   a. Spray an air freshener.

   b. Put a plant in the room

   c. Open a bedroom window.

   d. both b and c

2. Where is the best place to put a sun-loving plant inside a bedroom?

   a. under the bed

   b. inside a dark closet that is rarely opened

   c. near a window

   d. none of the above

3. Write an investigation to determine whether a houseplant could survive indoors with electric lighting only and no sunlight.

   _____

   _____

   _____

   _____

Name: _____ **Date:** _____

Directions: Draw the process of photosynthesis, and label you drawing.

Communicating Results

Name: _____ Date: _____

Directions: Read the text, and answer the questions.

The Digestive Process

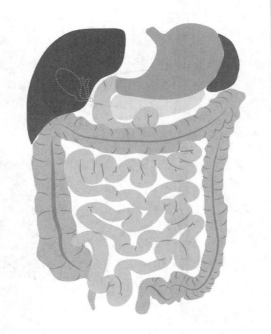

The digestive process breaks down the food you eat into useful *nutrients*. The blood in your circulatory system takes the nutrients to every cell in your body to give you energy.

The process of digestion begins in the mouth. Our teeth crush and grind food into smaller pieces. Our saliva mixes with chemicals called *enzymes* that break down starches into sugar. Then we swallow. The food travels through a muscular tube called the *esophagus*. It squeezes the food into the stomach. More enzymes make the food particles even smaller. Then they go into the small intestine to be broken down further by the liver, pancreas, and gallbladder. In the small intestine, nutrients, vitamins, minerals, and water are absorbed into the blood. It is then carried to every cell in the body to provide energy. Undigested fiber and water go to the large intestine (colon) and pass out of the body.

1. The digestive process begins _____ .

   a. in the stomach

   b. in the mouth

   c. in the colon

   d. in the small intestine

2. What is the muscular tube that squeezes food into the stomach?

   a. carbohydrate

   b. enzyme

   c. esophagus

   d. pancreas

3. What is the purpose of the small intestine?

   _____

   _____

   _____

   _____

Learning Content

Analyzing Data

Name: _____ **Date:** _____

Directions: Study the diagram of the digestive system. Then, answer the questions.

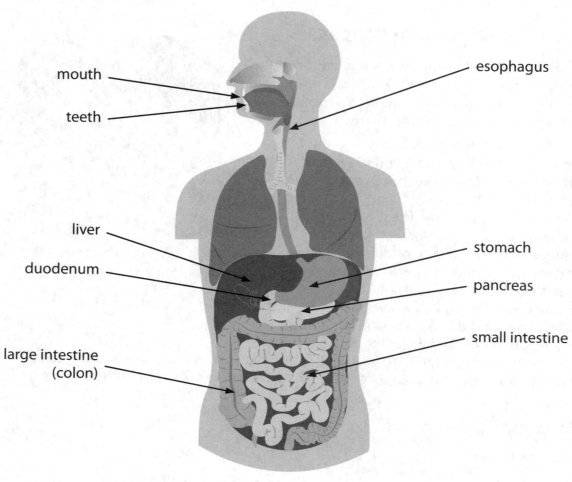

mouth

teeth

esophagus

liver

duodenum

stomach

pancreas

small intestine

large intestine
(colon)

1. The pancreas is located _____.

   a. in the large intestine   **b.** in the small intestine

   c. beside the esophagus   **d.** behind and under the stomach

2. What is another name for the large intestine?

   a. duodenum   **b.** colon

   c. gall bladder   **d.** rectal

3. What is the purpose of the esophagus?

   _____

   _____

Name: _____ **Date:** _____

Directions: Read the text, and answer the questions.

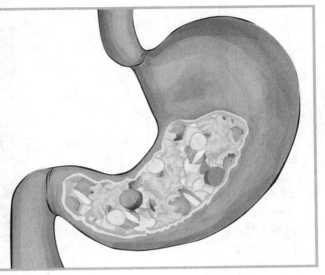

Carmen wants to become a doctor. She is interested in knowing more about the human body. She discovers that the stomach is not the place where digestion really happens. Instead, the stomach serves as a "waiting room" where food waits to be processed (digested). Most of the digestive process happens in the small intestine. Carmen also discovers that the liver processes the nutrients that are absorbed from the small intestine.

1. Where does most of the digestive process happen?

   a. the mouth

   b. the small intestine

   c. the esophagus

   d. the liver

2. What is the purpose of the liver?

   a. to send signals that the digestive process is starting

   b. to process waste absorbed from the esophagus

   c. to process nutrients absorbed from the small intestine

   d. to serve as a place where food waits to be digested.

3. What questions can Carmen ask about the digestive processes in other organs?

_____

_____

_____

_____

Planning Solutions

Name: _____   **Date:** _____

Directions: Read the text, and answer the question.

The hard-working small intestine is a thin tube, about one inch around, about 20 feet long, and coiled like a hose. The inside surface is full of many ridges and folds that help in the digestion of food and the absorption of nutrients.

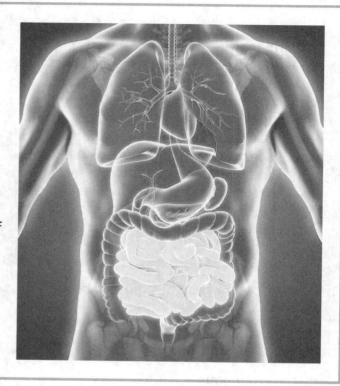

1. You want to show your class how long the small intestine is. Write how you would do this and what item or items you could use in your demonstration.

_____

_____

_____

_____

_____

_____

_____

_____

_____

_____

51412—180 Days of Science   © *Shell Education*

Name: _____ **Date:** _____

Directions: Using the information you've learned, briefly describe the function of the following:

1. Esophagus

_____

_____

_____

2. Stomach

_____

_____

_____

3. Small Intestine

_____

_____

_____

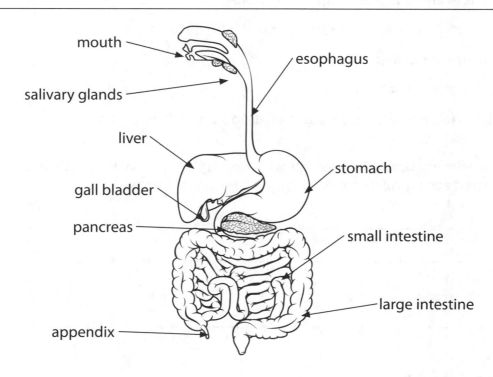

mouth

salivary glands

esophagus

liver

gall bladder

pancreas

stomach

small intestine

large intestine

appendix

ABC

Communicating Results

Name: _____ Date: _____

Directions: Read the text, and answer the questions.

The Ecosystem and Population Growth

An ecosystem includes all of the living and nonliving things in a specific environment. Most ecosystems include water, air, sunlight, soil, plants, microorganisms, insects and animals. Ecosystems may be on land or in water. Sizes of ecosystems may vary from small puddles to large tropical rain forests. Even a coral reef is an ecosystem.

Today more than seven billion people live on Earth. We all use products and services that are from nature. But problems arise when we use more than the Earth can renew. Studies show that we are using our natural resources too quickly. It takes one year and six months for Earth to recreate what we use in one year. This measurement is known as our "ecological footprint." It is a measurement of the land and water area required to produce everything we use, and to absorb our waste.

1. How long does it take Earth to reproduce what we are using in one year?

   a. one year and three months

   b. one year and six months

   c. two years

   d. four years

2. What does an ecological footprint measure?

   a. the difference between our planet and other planets

   b. the size of our feet

   c. the circumference of Earth

   d. the amount of land and water it takes to supply all we eat and use

3. If you were working with scientists who were trying to solve the problem of Earth's oversized ecological footprint, what would you tell them to do?

   _____

   _____

   _____

   _____

Name: _____ **Date:** _____

Directions: Read the text, study the chart, and answer the questions.

> Cities use huge amounts of food, energy, water, and materials. Farms and wildlands are being taken over by urban growth. Cities are growing larger, and moving into ecosystems where wild plants and animals thrive.
>
> In a famous essay, written in 1798, Reverend Thomas Malthus said that our population would grow faster than we could grow food. He said that eventually we would starve. That has not happened, but still, scientists are concerned.
>
> There are several levels of ecology that focus on all of these concerns from slightly different viewpoints.

Ecology	Definition
Organism Ecology	It is the study of adaptations and features that develop to allow organisms to live in certain habitats.
Population Ecology	It is the study of the size, density, and structure of populations, and their changes over time.
Community Ecology	It is the study of all the populations of different species and their interactions with one another, in a certain area.
Ecosystem Ecology	It is the study of all organisms, including non-living organisms, in an area. The flow of energy and the recycling of nutrients are part of this branch of ecology.
Biosphere Ecology	It is the study of Earth as an ecological system. The study may include interactions among ecosystems, climate change and other patterns that affect the entire globe.

1. Which branch of ecology focuses on the flow of energy and the recycling of nutrients?

   a. biosphere

   b. community

   c. ecosystem

   d. organism

2. Do you think Malthus's prediction might happen? Which sphere of ecology does his prediction concern?

   _____

   _____

Analyzing Data

Developing Questions

Name: _____   **Date:** _____

Directions: Read the text, and answer the questions.

> Jon is studying population growth and ecosystems. He begins to wonder if Malthus was right: that eventually people might starve if our population keeps growing. These are some things he has read.
>
> In 1968, Paul Ehrlich, a population biologist, wrote a book called *The Population Bomb*. He warned of mass starvation. He said that we are using all of our natural resources.
>
> Today there are about seven billion people on Earth. When we talk about population, it is not only about the number of people. It is about how we live, what we consume, and what we waste. Ehrlich was worried about our oceans and rivers, clean water supply, croplands, forests, wildlife, air quality, and weather.

1. Why did Ehrlich think we are heading for disaster?

   a. We are using up our natural resources.

   b. We are too busy.

   c. We have too much technology.

   d. We do not have enough technology.

2. What are some things we can all do to take care of our planet's resources?

   a. recycle

   b. turn off lights when not in use

   c. conserve water

   d. all of the above

3. What question could you ask about our ability to feed and sustain the planet?

   _____

   _____

   _____

   _____

Planning Solutions

Name: _____ **Date:** _____

Directions: Read the text, study the chart, and answer the questions.

> Jon lives in a tropical area near a creek. He takes walks there almost every day. As he continues studying ecosystems, he discovers five things that living organisms must have to support life.

The Basic Needs of Living Things	
sunlight	provides heat for animals and energy for plants
water	necessary for living cells and tissues to work
food	provides energy for moving, growing, and working
air	oxygen and carbon dioxide are necessary for survival
temperature	Whether on land or water, every living organism needs the right temperature for survival.

1. Where might Jon find an ecosystem to study, near his home?

   a. the grocery store nearby   **b.** the creek nearby

   c. the library nearby   **d.** the stadium nearby

2. What could Jon keep track of in his science journal as he studies the ecosystem near his home?

   a. the types of living organisms in the area   **b.** the amount of sunlight in the area

   c. the water level at different times of the year   **d.** all of the above

3. What experiment could Jon begin in the ecosystem near his home?

   _____

   _____

   _____

   _____

   _____

Communicating Results

Name: _____ **Date:** _____

Directions: Draw an ecosystem that includes at least five of the following things: land, water, living organisms, sunlight, food, plants, insects, and animals.

Name: _____   Date: _____

Directions: Read the text, and answer the questions.

Learning Content

Plant Reproduction

Plant reproduction is important to life on Earth. The first step in plant reproduction is pollination. Pollination happens when pollen grains go from one flowering plant to another. One way this can happen is by a pollinator. There are many pollinators. Bees, birds, and butterflies are pollinators. The wind and water are pollinators too. Pollinators transfer the pollen grains from one flowering plant to another. The pollen fertilizes egg cells to make new seeds. The seeds then grow to become new flowering plants.

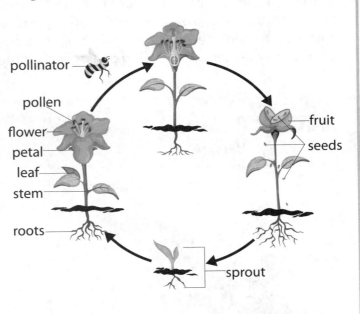

1. What is pollination?

   a. an important part of the life cycle of plants

   b. the process of pollen transfer

   c. the process of reproduction in plants

   d. all of the above

2. What do flowering plants depend on for reproduction?

   a. wind tunnels

   b. animals and wind

   c. flowers and wind

   d. soil and wind

3. How is the pollination of plants dependent on pollinators?

   _____

   _____

   _____

Analyzing Data

Name: _____ **Date:** _____

Directions: Read the text, study the images, and answer the questions.

Pollinators carry pollen in different ways. Birds and bats carry pollen in their feathers or hair. Invertebrates, like bees and butterflies, do not have hair. They have bristles on their legs, head, and other body parts. When a butterfly or bee uses its proboscis to drink nectar, it gets pollen on its proboscis and head. Bees also have tiny baskets on their legs for carrying pollen back to the hive.

Pollen Transfer	
Vertebrates	**Invertebrates**

hair
wings

bristles
head
pollen basket
proboscis

1. What does a proboscis do?

   a. It helps the leg.

   b. It's used by the bee to sip nectar.

   c. It's a bristle that stings the flower.

   d. It helps butterflies breathe.

2. How do bees and butterflies carry pollen?

   a. with bristles on their legs and head

   b. with small cone-shaped body parts

   c. with hair follicles

   d. none of the above

3. Bees use pollen baskets to _____ .

   a. carry pollen to the hive

   b. transfer pollen to flowering plants

   c. support the proboscis

   d. both a and b

Name: _____ Date: _____

Directions: Read the text, and answer the questions.

Birds like to drink the nectar of colorful flowers. Carmen visits her aunt in the country. Her aunt likes to feed hummingbirds. Carmen watches her aunt fill the red bird feeder with water and red food coloring. The food coloring makes the water turn red. Carmen wonders why her aunt adds food coloring to the water. The next day, Carmen sees hummingbirds outside drinking the red water.

1. Why do you think the hummingbirds were attracted to the water?

   a. They like red plants, so the red water attracted them.

   b. The water was warm, and that made them want a bath.

   c. They could smell the water.

   d. Hummingbirds only fly near red things.

2. What question can you ask about hummingbirds?

   _____

   _____

   _____

3. What question can you ask about empty bird feeders?

   _____

   _____

   _____

4. What question can you ask about white flowers?

   _____

   _____

   _____

Name: _____ **Date:** _____

Directions: Read the text, and answer the questions.

Larry plants tomato stems in his yard. Larry knows that tomatoes are pollinated by wind and, sometimes, by bees. After one year, the plants have very few tomatoes.

1. Why did Larry's plants yield so few tomatoes?

   a. The weather was too cold.

   b. There were too many bees in his yard.

   c. There was not enough pollination.

   d. all of the above

2. What could Larry do for his plants to yield more tomatoes?

   a. plant colorful flowers

   b. plant more tomato stems

   c. add a bird feeder to his yard

   d. add a fountain to his yard

3. What are some other things that Larry could try as he experiments with growing tomatoes?

   a. move his plants to a shaded area

   b. move his plants to a more windy area

   c. cut the stems of his plants

   d. add fertilizer to his plants

4. If you gave Larry a plant journal, what would you suggest that he write in it?

   _____

   _____

Name: _____ **Date:** _____

Directions: Use the word bank to complete the sentences.

bees	proboscis
plant reproduction	red
pollen	wind
pollination	

1. _____ is crucial to life on our planet.

2. The first step in plant reproduction is _____ .

3. Animal pollinators carry _____ in different ways.

4. A butterfly or a bee uses its long, thin _____ to sip nectar from flowers.

5. _____ have tiny baskets on their legs for carrying pollen back to the hive.

6. Hummingbirds are particularly attracted to the color _____ .

7. Tomatoes rely on _____ for pollination.

Learning Content

Name: _____ **Date:** _____

Directions: Read the text, and answer the questions.

Environmental and Genetic Factors

We all have traits that make us unique. Some of our traits, like height, hair color, and eye color are controlled by genes. We inherit genes from our parents. Other traits are shaped by our environment. These include our culture, experiences, and surroundings. For example, we are not born with the ability to speak a certain language. We learn to speak the language we hear every day. Our traits are influenced by both our environment and our genetics. For example, our height and weight is influenced by our parents, but it is also influenced by our nutrition. The genes we received from our parents and our experiences make us who we are.

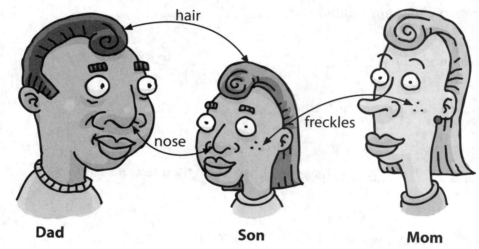

Dad   **Son**   **Mom**

1. What does our environment include?

   a. our eye color and hair color

   b. our ear shape and foot size

   c. our culture, experiences, and surroundings

   d. inherited traits we received from our parents

2. What is an inherited trait?

   a. the language we speak

   b. the experiences we have

   c. the color of our hair

   d. something that cannot be seen

3. What trait is influenced by both environment and genetics?

   a. weight

   b. height

   c. eye color

   d. both a and b

Name: _____ **Date:** _____

Directions: Study the chart, and answer the questions.

Every living organism requires a set of instructions for specifying its traits. Heredity is the passage of these genetic instructions from parents to children. This information is contained in genes, located in the chromosomes of each cell. Each gene carries a single unit of information that determines one biological characteristic. Each gene is composed of DNA, the chemical basis of heredity that is passed on from parents to children.

Traits		
Trait	Inherited	Acquired
face shape	X	
eye color	X	
hair color	X	
large, exercised muscles		X
good ballet skills		X
good bike rider		X
dimples	X	
long legs	X	
small nose	X	

1. An inherited trait includes _____ .

   a. long fingernails   **b.** sore muscles

   c. long legs   **d.** a long moustache

2. Which of the following acquired traits can also be influenced by genetics?

   a. large, exercised muscles   **b.** good ballet skills

   c. good bike rider   **d.** both b and c

Name: _____ **Date:** _____

Directions: Read the text, and answer the questions.

Samira notices that she and her friend Lena talk the same way. Samira notices they have the same accent. She also notices that she looks very different from Lena. Samira is short with straight blond hair. Lena is tall and has dark, curly hair.

1. Which trait of both Samira's and Lena's is a product of their environment?

    a. color of their hair

    b. shape of their hair

    c. height

    d. accent

2. What question could Samira and Lena ask about their similarities?

    _____

    _____

3. What question could Samira and Lena have about their differences?

    _____

    _____

4. What question could the girls ask one another about their environments?

    _____

    _____

Name: _____ **Date:** _____

Directions: Read the text, and answer the questions.

Agnes cannot roll her tongue, no matter how hard she tries. Sergei has always been able to roll his tongue. He doesn't even need to try. It comes naturally to him. Tongue rolling is controlled by an inherited gene. But, some people can learn how to roll their tongues. So environmental factors—not just genes—can influence the trait. Sergei is sure his trait is inherited.

1. Why do you think Sergei is so certain that he inherited the trait of tongue rolling rather than learning, or acquiring, the ability?

   a. He did not try to learn it; it was natural.

   b. He cannot do anything else that is interesting.

   c. He can do a lot of unusual things.

   d. none of the above

2. How can you learn about inherited or acquired tongue-rolling skills by interviewing your classmates? Write a plan to survey your class.

   _____

   _____

   _____

3. What other traits could you survey your class about? Write a plan.

   _____

   _____

   _____

   _____

Planning Solutions

Name: _____ **Date:** _____

Directions: Complete the chart with your unique traits, such as eye color, hair color, language, height, and abilities (such as dancing, sports, art, or anything you enjoy). Mark to show whether you think each trait was inherited, influenced by the environment, or both.

My Traits	Parents	Environment
eye color	X	

Communicating Results

Learning Content

Name: _____   **Date:** _____

Directions: Read the text, and answer the questions.

Fossils

Body fossils are the most common type of fossil. Body fossils are the remains of dead plants and animals in rock. Body fossils can be whole-body fossils or trace fossils. Whole-body fossils can be bones, teeth, or shells trapped in amber. Amber is fossilized tree resin. Trace fossils can be footprints, burrows, eggshells, nests, and teeth marks. Trace fossils provide clues to an organism's diet and behavior. Footprints can show the number of toes and the distance between its steps. Fossils give paleontologists a glimpse into life millions of years ago. Paleontologists are scientists who study fossils.

trace fossil   **body fossil**

1. The fossil of a footprint, burrow, or nest is called what?

   a. microbe

   b. trace fossil

   c. old fossil

   d. body fossil

2. What is a paleontologist?

   a. a history professor

   b. a scientist who studies biology

   c. a scientist who studies fossils

   d. a scientist who studies physics

3. What would a paleontologist want to know about a fossil that has just been discovered?

   _____

   _____

Analyzing Data

Name: _____ Date: _____

Directions: Read the text, study the chart, and answer the questions.

Trace fossils record activities of animals and plants when they were alive. Impressions are a type of trace fossil. Leaves are the most common fossils preserved as impressions. Footprint tracks can show the shape and size of the foot. They can also show if the organism had two feet or four feet.

Fossil	Description
tracks	made by moving organisms with feet/legs
trails	made by moving organisms without feet/legs
burrows	made by organisms digging in earth/mud
borings/tunnels	made by organisms digging in wood/rock
leaf impressions	made by a decomposed leaf

1. Burrows are impressions left by organisms that dug in _____ .

    a. wood   **b.** earth

    c. rock   **d.** snow

2. Which impressions are left by moving organisms?

    a. burrows   **b.** tracks

    c. trails   **d.** all of the above

3. What might you learn from an animal trail preserved as a trace fossil?

    _____

    _____

    _____

Name: _____ **Date:** _____

Directions: Read the text, and answer the questions.

A paleontologist visits Sadie's class. The paleontologist talks about how he studies fossils. He says all fossils are called the fossil record. The fossil record is like a history of Earth. It gives scientists clues about animals and plants that existed many, many years ago.

body fossil

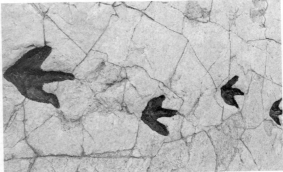

trace fossil

1. What can scientists learn from the fossil record?

   a. the kinds of plants and animals that once existed

   b. a history of life on Earth

   c. what will happen in the future

   d. both a and b

2. What question could Sadie ask about plants and animals that existed many years ago?

   _____

   _____

   _____

3. What question could Sadie ask Dr. Guerra about fossils?

   _____

   _____

   _____

Developing Questions

Planning Solutions

Name: _____ **Date:** _____

Directions: Read the text, and answer the questions.

Caroline got a gift from her aunt when she visited her in the summer. The gift looked like a smooth, honey-colored rock. Inside was a fossilized insect. Caroline's aunt told her the insect stepped in sticky tree resin many, many years ago. The insect couldn't escape and eventually got covered in sticky resin. After millions of years, the resin hardened into amber. Caroline brought the amber to class to show her friends.

1. What is amber made from?

   a. sticky glue

   b. tree leaves

   c. tree resin

   d. colored honey

2. What can we learn about by studying insects trapped in amber?

   a. organisms that lived here before we did

   b. organisms that lived in pre-historic eras

   c. organisms that roamed the Earth

   d. all of the above

3. Write the steps Caroline would take to show her class how amber is formed with an insect trapped inside.

   _____

   _____

   _____

   _____

Name: _____ **Date:** _____

Directions: Read the text. Then, fill in the blanks, putting the steps in the correct order, to explain how a fish becomes a fossil. Some blanks are already filled in for you.

When a fish dies, it sinks to the ocean floor. Its soft parts rot away leaving behind the skeleton. The skeleton is buried by mud and layers of sediment. The bones and sediment harden into rock. Over many years, water dissolves the rock leaving a skeleton-shaped hole. This is a natural mold. Mineral-rich water fills the mold and it becomes a skeleton-shaped cast stone. Often, the rock surrounding the fossil rises to the Earth's surface. Then the rock is worn away by wind and rain and the fossil is exposed.

ABC

Communicating Results

1. A fish dies.

2. _____

3. _____

4. Skeleton buried by mud.

5. Bones harden into rock.

6. _____

7. _____

8. _____

9. The rock is worn away by wind and rain and the fossil is exposed.

Learning Content

Name: _____ Date: _____

Directions: Read the text, and answer the questions.

Life of a Fossil

The ocean floor is called the "benthic zone." A benthic zone close to land is a good place for fossilization to take place. Sediment from land enters the ocean and covers dead organisms. In rainforests, it's hard for organisms to become fossilized because it rains so much. The wet weather breaks down tissues in organisms very quickly in the rainforest. Scavengers and decomposers also break down tissues quickly in the rainforest.

1. Why is the rain forest an unlikely place to find fossils?

   a. rain causes rapid decay of dead organisms

   b. decomposers quickly break down dead organisms

   c. both a and b

   d. sediment covers dead organisms

2. What is the benthic zone?

   a. land sediment

   b. the ocean floor

   c. the rainforest

   d. the ocean

3. Why is the benthic zone closest to land a good place for fossilization to take place?

   _____

   _____

   _____

   _____

Analyzing Data

Name: _____ **Date:** _____

Directions: Read the text, and study the chart. Answer the questions.

> Less than 10 percent of living things will become fossils. Animals with backbones, or vertebrates, have a better chance of becoming fossils than insects. That's because insects do not preserve well. When an animal is buried in sedimentary rock, it still might not become a fossil for many reasons. The rock might be buried too deep and melt because of extreme heat and pressure. Even if a fossil is formed, many things can destroy it.

Fossils do not form because…	Fossils can be destroyed if…
bodies are eaten by scavengers.	they are washed away.
bodies are decomposed by microorganisms.	they are moved by glaciers.
rain decays bodies quickly.	they are crushed in rockslides.
bones melt from heat and pressure.	they are eroded by weather.

1. What could prevent a fossil from forming?

   a. extreme heat

   b. decomposition

   c. rockslides

   d. both a and b

2. What could destroy a fossil after it has formed?

   a. extreme pressure

   b. erosion

   c. moving glaciers

   d. both b and c

3. What happens to animals that do not become fossils?

   _____

   _____

   _____

Developing Questions

Name: _____   **Date:** _____

Directions: Read the text, and answer the questions.

Jayna's dad has been collecting fossils from all over the world for many years. Jayna and her dad take the fossils to a professor to show him. The professor says the fossils are from animals that are now extinct. He says the fossil record is important because scientists get to study the differences between living animals and extinct animals. The professor tells them that the earliest known fossils are bacteria. Bacteria are one-celled organisms.

1. Jayna's dad's fossil record can allow scientists to study animals that are _____ .

   a. important

   b. endangered

   c. living and extinct

   d. both a and b

2. What's a question Jayna can ask about her dad's fossil record?

   _____

   _____

   _____

3. What question could Jayna ask about extinct animals?

   _____

   _____

   _____

Name: _____ **Date:** _____

Directions: Read the text, and answer the questions.

> The fossil record shows how many kinds of extinct organisms are very different from organisms that are living now. Scientists have also found that the skeletons of turtles, horses, birds, and bats are similar, despite their obvious differences. You and your friends study a fossil. You think the fossil is similar to a horse. Your friends disagree. They think it looks like a turtle.

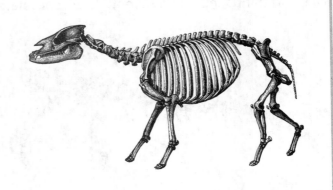

Planning Solutions

1. How would you discuss the subject with your friends?

   a. find pictures of horse skeletons to compare with the fossil

   b. try to discover where the fossil was found

   c. try to discover the kind of habitat where the fossilized creature lived

   d. all of the above

2. After you compare the fossil with the horse skeleton, what else would you do?

   a. focus on arguing your point

   b. compare the turtle with the fossil, just as you did with the horse

   c. call everyone before the meeting, and tell them you are right

   d. all of the above

3. What could you do to find out more about the differences between extinct animals and animals that are alive today?

   _____

   _____

   _____

   _____

   _____

Name: _____ **Date:** _____

Communicating Results

ABC

Directions: You are a paleontologist. Your job is to compare a body fossil of an extinct Tyrannosaurus Rex dinosaur with a horse that you might see today. Look for things that are alike and things that are different. Then, complete the chart.

	Tyrannosaurus Rex	**Horse**
size		
body		
back		
legs		
tail		
face		
hands		

Name: _____ **Date:** _____

Directions: Read the text, and answer the questions.

Unity and Diversity in Life

The basic elements of all living organisms are cells. Organisms work with one another in interacting systems. Think of it this way. Your thumb is useful to you as part of your hand, but a thumb unattached to a hand is useless.

You are unique, but you also have biological, chemical, and physical characteristics in common with other organisms. Since all cells work in a similar way, all organisms work in similar ways. Even bacteria and humans share some similarities.

In all living things, there are also differences; things that make us unique. This is true in every natural population, and between species. We are all alike in some ways, and we are different in some ways.

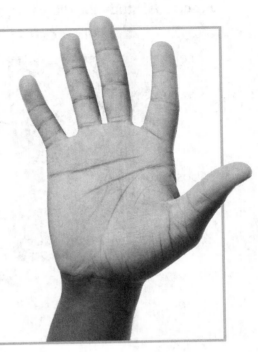

Learning Content

1. Organisms work with one another in _____ .

   a. interacting systems

   b. sync

   c. harmony

   d. none of the above

2. The basic functioning of all organisms is _____ .

   a. unrelated

   b. completely different

   c. similar

   d. like a thumb

3. What does the phrase, "We are all alike, and we are all different," mean to you?

   _____

   _____

   _____

   _____

Analyzing Data

Name: _____   Date: _____

Directions: Study the diagrams, and answer the questions.

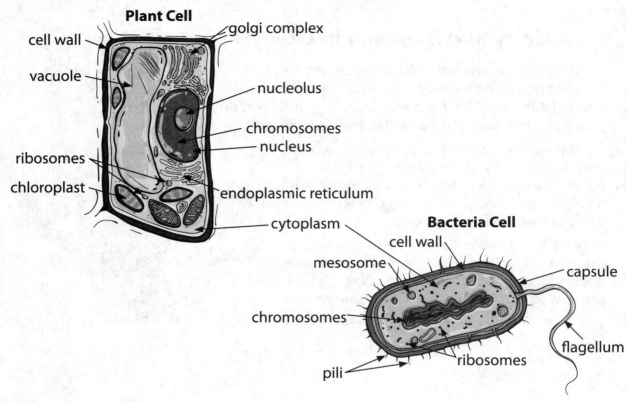

1. What similarities do you see between the plant and bacteria cells?

   a. cytoplasm in both   **b.** chromosomes in both

   c. ribosomes in both   **d.** all of the above

2. Which cell does not have a golgi complex?

   a. plant cell   **b.** bacteria cell

   c. animal cell   **d.** both a and b

3. If you could look at a cell under a microscope, how would you know whether it was a plant cell or bacteria cell?

   a. if there was no vacuole, it would be a bacteria cell

   b. if there were flagella, it would be a bacteria cell

   c. if there was chloroplast, it would be a plant cell

   d. all of the above

Name: _____ Date: _____

Directions: Read the text, and answer the questions.

Erica wants to be a biologist. Her class went to the zoo and to a wildflower garden last week. She learned that there are between five million and 10 million existing animal and plant species. She also learned that the first person who tried to create a scientific classification of plants and animals was the Greek philosopher, Aristotle. He wanted to show the relationship of all things to each other. This type of study is called ecology, and it is a branch of biology.

1. Who first attempted the scientific classification of organisms?

   a. Sophocles

   b. Aristotle

   c. Plato

   d. Erica

2. The study of the relationship of all things to each other is known as _____.

   a. immunology

   b. psychology

   c. ecology

   d. numerology

3. Write a question you might ask about ecology.

   _____

   _____

   _____

Developing Questions

Name: _____ Date: _____

Directions: Read the text. In the chart, name the parts that make the whole.

Mrs. Guerra told her students that atoms and cells make up all living things. In human beings, many cells make up one system, and many systems work together to keep us alive. She gave an example: A human being cannot breathe without a respiratory system. She asked the class to investigate this concept. They were to think of non-human examples to show that several things together make one whole thing. Mary Ellen said that certain colors, all put together, make one rainbow. This is the list that the students created.

	Parts That Make One Whole
star	gas
bicycle	wheel
tree	
clock	
ferris wheel	
table	
chair	
mountain	
blue jeans	

Planning Solutions

Name: _____   **Date:** _____

Communicating Results

Directions: Draw one whole apple. Write the names of the parts of the apple that you can see. Then, draw an apple that is cut in half. Write the names of the apple parts that you can see now.

ABC

1. Look at the two pictures you have drawn. When the apple is whole, how many parts of the apple can you see?

   _____

2. When the apple is cut in half, how many parts of the apple can you see?

   _____

3. Write a sentence about what you have learned about parts that make up one whole thing.

   _____

   _____

Learning Content

Name: _____ **Date:** _____

Directions: Read the text, and answer the questions.

Living Things and the Environment

Very big changes within an ecosystem will affect the organisms living there. Think about what might happen to a polar bear if the temperature in the arctic became very warm. What might happen to a frog in a lake if the lake dried up? When changes in the environment happen, the species (in these examples, polar bear or frog) must adapt or migrate to another area, in order to survive. To adapt means to adjust to new conditions. To migrate means to move from one type of place to another.

We know that ducks and geese fly south to avoid their cold northern winters. Then in summer, they return home to the north. This is seasonal migration. Permanent migration, also known as forced migration, means that there is no return to the original home.

A species is in danger of extinction (dying out, vanishing) if it does not adapt to changing conditions such as new food sources, new predators, or drastic weather changes. Extinction refers to the disappearance of an entire species of animals, not just one animal.

1. What does the word "migrate" mean?

   a. to stay where you are

   b. to move from one type of place to another

   c. to adjust to new conditions

   d. big changes within an ecosystem

2. What is another term for permanent migration?

   a. good migration

   b. distant migration

   c. forced migration

   d. bad migration

3. Why might populations of animals migrate to other types of areas?

_____

_____

_____

_____

Name: _____   **Date:** _____

Directions: Study the food web below. It shows how various species of plants and animals are dependent on one another for food. Answer the questions.

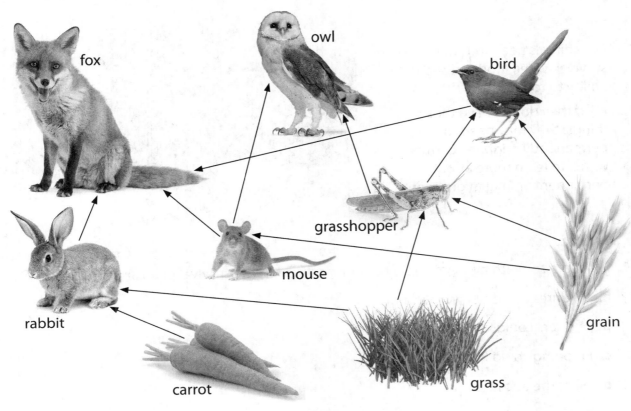

1. What is the owl directly dependent upon for its food source?

   a. rabbits and carrots

   c. birds and rabbits

   b. grasshoppers and mice

   d. grasshoppers and carrots

2. If one food source disappeared, why would the fox have a better chance of survival than other animals?

   a. He is scarier.

   c. He has three food sources: rabbits, mice and birds.

   b. He has more fur.

   d. He has three food sources: grass, birds, and grains.

3. How does this affect your view of the way we take care of our planet and its inhabitants?

   _____

   _____

Name: _____ **Date:** _____

Developing Questions

Directions: Read the text, and answer the questions.

Animals need four things to survive: water, food, air, and the ability to reproduce.

If they do not have these things, they may need to permanently migrate. Carmen wants to learn more about permanent animal migrations.

1. What are some things that could happen to threaten the survival of an animal species?

   a. Wildfires could burn vegetation.

   b. Hunters could kill animal mates.

   c. Flooding could kill animal mates.

   d. all of the above

2. What are four things that an animal population needs to survive?

   a. water, land, rivers, and ability to reproduce

   b. water, rivers, air, and a mild climate

   c. water, grass, food, and a place to hide

   d. water, food, air, and ability to reproduce

3. What is a question you have about migration?

   _____

   _____

   _____

Name: _____   **Date:** _____

Directions: Read the text, and answer the questions.

> Kara's class is studying learned behaviors and instinctive (innate) behaviors. Her assignment is to write about what she has learned this semester. This is what she has written.
>
> In the animal kingdom, instinctive behavior is a mystery. A spider knows how to spin a web. A bird knows how to build a nest. A turtle buries her eggs. These behaviors are not taught. They are inherited. The animals simply do "what comes naturally." Baby ducklings crouch when predators fly overhead, but they do not crouch when other ducks fly over. Learned behaviors are different from innate behaviors. Learned behaviors happen during one's lifetime. Learned behaviors are also called acquired behaviors. A dog can be taught to shake hands. A chimp can learn to use tools.

1. An innate behavior is _____ .

   a. inherited

   b. instinctive

   c. unhealthy

   d. both a and b

2. A learned behavior is also called _____ .

   a. innate

   b. something that causes a specific reaction

   c. acquired

   d. seasonal

3. When a baby duckling hatches, it does not know that it is a duck. It will visually "imprint" on the first living creature it sees that is larger than itself. It will identify only with that species for the rest of its life. What question could you ask about imprinting?

_____

_____

_____

Planning Solutions

Communicating Results

Name: _____ **Date:** _____

Directions: Draw a line from each word to its meaning. Then, answer the question.

migrate ●   ● inherited

permanent migration ●   ● characteristic

seasonal migration ●   ● to identify with a certain
                                                  species for life

innate ●   ● acquired behavior

trait ●   ● to move from one type
                                                  of place to another

imprinting ●   ● leaving in summer, and
                                                  returning in winter

learned behavior ●   ● to never return to the
                                                  original home

1. What is an acquired ability that a family dog might have?

_____

_____

Name: _____ Date: _____

Directions: Read the text, and answer the questions.

Adapting in the Wild

Imagine that green geckos are living in a green forest. They are almost never caught by predators because they look just like green plants, and predators can't see them. In the same green forest, red geckos are easy targets because any predator can see them, grab them, and have them for lunch. As time passes, very few red geckoes are left, and green geckoes are everywhere. This process is called *natural selection*. Organisms that are adapted to their environment tend to survive.

1. What is natural selection?

   a. permanent or seasonal migration

   b. growing to adulthood

   c. adapting to one's environment to survive

   d. photosynthesis and other processes

2. What does it mean to adapt?

   a. to try

   b. to do one's best

   c. to adjust to a situation

   d. to disappear

3. In order to survive as a population, what adaptations would have helped the red geckos?

   _____

   _____

   _____

Learning Content

Analyzing Data

Name: _____ Date: _____

Directions: Read the text, and study the chart. Answer the questions.

Many different types of animals live in habitats all over the world. Their physical bodies are adapted to help them survive in their environments. Physical changes, however, do not happen over a short period of time. Adaptations happen very slowly over generations. The following chart shows the physical adaptations of the camel, penguin, and giraffe.

Animal Adaptations		
Animal	**Habitat**	**Adaptations**
camel	hot sandy desert	Thick eyelashes and eyebrows keep sand out of their eyes. The ability to close their nostrils keeps sand out of their noses. Tan color allows them to blend in with sandy, desert colors.
penguin	cold Antarctic	Outer feathers are waterproof; inner feathers provide insulation for warmth. Dark feathers absorb light from the sun. Their thick skin has blubber underneath for warmth.
giraffe	warm, sunny African savannas	The giraffe's neck is six feet long and perfect for eating leaves from the tops of trees. The tongue is long and leathery to protect against thorns when eating. The spotted color is camouflage from predators.

1. Which animals are adapted to warmer climates?

   a. penguin and camel

   b. penguin and giraffe

   c. camel and giraffe

   d. all of the above

2. How does the penguin stay warm?

   a. jumping and running

   b. running, climbing, and swimming

   c. feathers, thick skin, and blubber

   d. alternating between standing and walking

3. Write two ways the camel is adapted to life in the desert.

   _____

   _____

Name: _____   **Date:** _____

Directions: Read the text, and answer the questions.

Lucy is on a hiking trip with her dad. Lucy notices a ladybug hidden on a flower. Lucy's dad tells her that is how it stays safe. It is using camouflage to hide from predators. Lucy asks how the ladybug hides in winter when there are not flowers. Lucy's dad says that they hibernate. The ladybug uses two types of adaptation to survive; camouflage and hibernations. Lucy tells her dad she knows other animals that hibernate. They are groundhogs, bears, and hummingbirds.

1. Name another animal other than the ladybug that hibernates?

   a. bear   **b.** rabbits

   c. skunk   **d.** deer

2. What adaptation do ladybugs use when the flowers are in bloom?

   a. camouflage   **b.** fly south

   c. hibernation   **d.** none of the above

3. What question could you ask about animal adaptation?

   _____

   _____

   _____

   _____

Developing Questions

Name: _____ **Date:** _____

Directions: Read the text, and answer the questions.

> Dillon is studying animal adaptations. He is beginning a research paper. He knows that adaptation helps an organism, such as a plant or animal, to survive in its environment. An adaptation can be a physical part of the organism. An adaptation can also be the way an organism behaves, or acts.
>
> Dillon will be writing about these animal adaptations:
>
> - Sea turtle: fins for swimming
> - Tortoise: hard protective shell
> - Fish: eyes on sides of head to see predators
> - Crab: can move sideways to escape predators
> - Camel: thick, leathery tongue to eat cacti
> - Elephant: big ears and tail to swat flies
> - Grasshopper: legs for jumping
> - Fish: gills
> - Penguins: has waterproof feathers to keep warm
> - Whale: has a blowhole
> - Giraffe: long neck to eat leaves from tops of trees

1. Which of these are physical adaptations of animals?

    a. eyes on sides of head

    b. fingernails

    c. thick skin; leathery tongue

    d. both a and c

2. What animal could Dillion observe to test camouflage?

    a. green gecko

    b. hyena

    c. ant

    d. cat

Name: _____ **Date:** _____

Directions: Read each sentence. Write the name of an animal that has each type of adaptation.

hard protective shell	
eyes on the side of its head	
lives in the desert and has a thick, leathery tongue	
big ears and a big tail to swat flies	
has gills	
has waterproof feathers to keep warm	
with fins	
a neck that is six feet long to reach leaves from tall trees	
a mammal and has a blowhole to breathe in water	
has legs for jumping quickly	

Communicating Results

ABC

Name: _____ **Date:** _____

Directions: Read the text, and answer the questions.

Atoms

Everything in the universe is made of matter—trees, clothes, the air, and you! Matter is anything that has mass and takes up space. Atoms are the basic building blocks of all matter. Atoms are made of three basic particles: protons, neutrons, and electrons. Protons and neutrons join together to form the nucleus, and electrons orbit the nucleus. An element is a substance that is made entirely from one type of atom. For example, the element hydrogen is made from atoms containing just one proton and one electron.

1. What are atoms made of?

   a. electrical neutrons and matter

   b. protons and matter

   c. protons, neutrons, and electrons

   d. none of the above

2. What are the building blocks of matter?

   a. protons

   b. atoms

   c. electrons

   d. element

3. Why do you think scientists study atoms?

   _____

   _____

   _____

   _____

Name: _____   **Date:** _____

Directions: Read the text, study the chart, and answer the questions.

It is hard to imagine how small an atom is. But let's try. Imagine that an atom were the size of a blueberry, and we wanted to see how many atoms were in a grapefruit, the grapefruit would have to be the size of planet Earth to fit all those blueberries.

Clearly, atoms are very, very small. Do you want further proof? Take a look at this chart.

How Many Atoms Are in a Human?	
Weight	154 pounds
Atoms	7,000,000,000,000,000,000,000,000,000

Atoms are the smallest amount of something called an *element*. Hydrogen is a type of element, for example. Each element is made of only one type of atom. There are 118 different types of elements.

1. How many atoms are in a human?

   a. 7,000,000,000,000,000,000

   b. 118

   c. 7,000,000,000,000

   d. 7,000,000,000,000,000,000,000,000,000

2. Atoms are the smallest part of _____.

   a. elements

   b. electrons

   c. protons

   d. neutrons

3. What kinds of things can you learn from studying atoms?

   _____

   _____

   _____

Name: _____   **Date:** _____

Developing Questions

Directions: Read the text, and answer the questions.

Miss Jackson's class is learning about atoms. Everyone has a different assignment. Lisa reports that atoms are made of protons, neutrons, and electrons. Jason reads to the class, "There are 118 kinds of elements, and each one has a name." Javier explains that all known elements are arranged on a chart called the Periodic Table of Elements. He says that each element has its own unique atomic number that tells the number of protons it has.

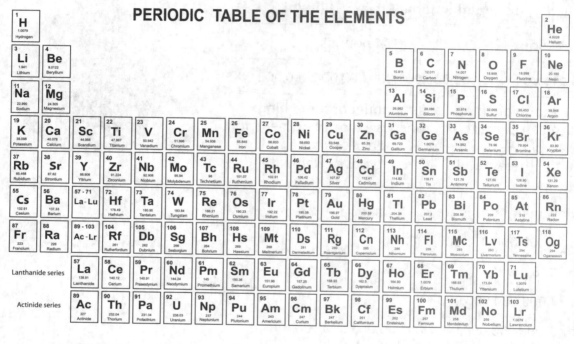

PERIODIC TABLE OF THE ELEMENTS

1. What are: gold, silver, copper, and carbon?

   a. protons

   b. iron

   c. elements

   d. nitrogen

2. Look at the chart and find the atomic number element 118. What is the symbol?

   a. Og

   b. Sc

   c. Xe

   d. Gl

3. Write a question about the Periodic Table of Elements.

   _____

   _____

Name: _____ **Date:** _____

Directions: Read the text, study the chart, and answer the questions.

> Mr. Chase's class was studying the Periodic Table of Elements. He put a chart on the board, showing the six elements that make up 99% of the human body.

Main Elements of the Human Body	
O—oxygen	65.0%
C—carbon	18.5%
H—hydrogen	9.5%
N—nitrogen	3.2%
Ca—calcium	1.5%
P—phosphorus	1.2%

1. What element makes up most of your body?

   a. oxygen

   b. nitrogen

   c. sodium

   d. chlorine

2. What percentage of your body is made up of carbon?

   a. 65%

   b. 18.5%

   c. 1.5%

   d. 3.2%

3. How can you learn more about elements?

   _____

   _____

Planning Solutions

Communicating Results

Name: _____ Date: _____

Directions: Use the word bank to answer the questions.

atoms	hydrogen	nitrogen	118
calcium	hydrogen	oxygen	242
carbon	matter	phosphorous	
electrons	neutrons	protons	

1. Everything in the universe is made of what? _____

2. What are the building blocks of matter? _____

3. What three basic particles are atoms made of?

_____

_____

_____

4. From the Periodic Table, which element does the symbol H represent? _____

5. How many elements are in the Periodic Table? _____

6. Name at least three of the six main elements that make up the human body.

_____

_____

_____

_____

Name: _____ **Date:** _____

Directions: Read the text, and answer the questions.

Physical Changes

What is a physical change? Think of holding a cup of water. The water in the cup is a liquid, and you can drink it. But suppose you put it in the freezer. The water freezes and becomes ice. Is the ice still water? Yes. It has simply had a physical change. Now, suppose you allow the ice to melt back into liquid. This is another physical change. If you boil it and create steam, this will also be a physical change. Is the steam still water? Yes.

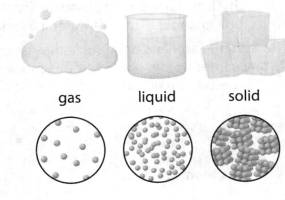

gas   liquid   solid

In seeing the water change from liquid to ice, back to liquid, and then to steam, what was really changing? The form of the water. The form of the water can also be called the state of water. The formula for water is H_2O: two hydrogen atoms and one oxygen atom. If a substance undergoes a change, and its formula remains the same, the change is physical.

Sometimes, a physical change can be reversed. It is easy to reverse the form of water. However, not all physical changes are reversible.

1. In a physical change, what changes?

   a. the form, or state, of the substance

   b. the formula of the substance

   c. the sign of the substance

   d. none of the above

2. What is the formula for water?

   a. P_2O

   b. H_3O

   c. H_2O

   d. HO_2

3. Describe the scientific reasons that crushing a can is a physical change.

   _____

   _____

   _____

Analyzing Data

Name: _____ **Date:** _____

Directions: Read the text, study the chart,

In a physical change, the substance continues to be the same substance that it was; only its form changes. Think of water as liquid, ice, and steam.

In a chemical change, the substance changes into something else. The original substance loses its identity. Something new is created. Think of burning a piece of wood. It becomes a pile of ashes. It is no longer wood.

Chemical vs Physical Change	
Chemical Change	**Physical Change**
Was cooking involved?	Did the shape change?
Was burning involved?	Did something dissolve in water?
Was there an explosion?	Did something melt?
Was there smoke or ashes?	Did something freeze?
Were there gas bubbles?	Did something evaporate?
Did the change create a new substance?	Did the form of the substance change?
Change cannot be reversed.	Change can be reversed.

1. If cooking or burning are involved, what kind of change is made?

   a. physical   **b.** chemical

   c. kitchen   **d.** none of the above

2. What could you do to create a physical change?

   a. Cut paper in two.   **b.** Bake a cake.

   c. Shoot firecrackers.   **d.** Burn wood.

3. What can you learn from physical and chemical changes?

_____

_____

_____

_____

Physical Science

Name: _____ **Date:** _____

Directions: Read the text, study the chart, and answer the questions.

> To show the result of a chemical change, Mrs. Martine brought a rusted steel garbage can to class. The iron (Fe) in the metal combined with oxygen (O_2) in the atmosphere to create a new substance: iron oxide, or rust (Fe_2O_3).
>
> She said that sometimes when a chemical change is taking place, there may be fizzy bubbles or a color change. An explosion might even happen. Chemical changes cannot be reversed.
>
> Peggy asked Mrs. Martine for another example of a chemical change. Mrs. Martine said that baking a cake is a chemical change. Sugar, salt, milk, and butter are mixed and baked to become a cake. So they are no longer the individual ingredients they were.

Physical Changes	Chemical Changes
Aluminum foil is cut in half.	Milk goes sour.
Clay is molded into a new shape.	Jewelry tarnishes.
Butter melts on warm toast.	Bread becomes toast.
Water evaporates from the surface of the ocean.	Rust forms on a nail.

1. Chemical changes cannot be _____ .

   a. completed   **b.** difficult

   c. easy   **d.** reversed

2. A chemical change creates a _____ .

   a. new substance   **b.** bad result

   c. good result   **d.** messy substance

3. Write a question you might ask about physical or chemical changes.

_____

_____

_____

Developing Questions

Name: _____ Date: _____

Directions: Read the text, and answer the questions.

> After studying about physical and chemical changes, Jaden asked permission to do an experiment at home. In the kitchen, he poured a small amount of vinegar into a cup. He added one tablespoon of baking soda. It fizzed and bubbled. He concluded that he had created a chemical change.
>
> These are examples of chemical changes:
> - exploding fireworks
> - rotting bananas
> - grilling hamburgers
> - burning wood
> - digesting food
> - cooking eggs
> - baking cakes

1. Why can't chemical changes be reversed?

a. They are too complicated.

b. It takes too long.

c. The materials are worn out.

d. A new substance has already been created.

2. From the list above, which changes do not require cooking or high heat?

a. rotting bananas

b. digesting food

c. exploding fireworks

d. both a and b

3. What experiment could you do to compare the difference between a physical change and a chemical change?

_____

_____

_____

Name: _____   Date: _____

Directions: Study the chart. Indicate whether each activity is a physical or chemical change.

Activity	Result	Physical or Chemical Change
Crush a can.	shape change/size	
Change the shape of clay.	shape change/size	
Rip a piece of paper.	shape change/size	
Burn a piece of paper.	fire/heat/light	
Get paper wet.	mixture	
Add Alka-Seltzer to water.	fizzy bubbles	
Melt ice.	change in form	
Burn fireworks.	color changes/fire	
Make bread from dough.	color change/ shape change	
Add baking soda to vinegar.	fizz/heat	
Burn a candle.	light/heat	
Heat sugar to make caramel.	heat/color change/ shape change	

ABC

Communicating Results

Learning Content

Name: _____   **Date:** _____

Directions: Read the text, study the infographic, and answer the questions.

Natural Resources

Natural resources are substances such as minerals, forests, fresh water, and fertile land that are found in nature and are necessary or useful for sustaining human populations. All substances in our world, including synthetic products that are human-made, originally came from plants and animals. For example, plastic is a synthetic material made from petroleum, which is a natural resource pumped out of the ground.

The process of changing natural resources into synthetic products, such as plastics, medicines, and fuels, is called *chemical synthesis*.

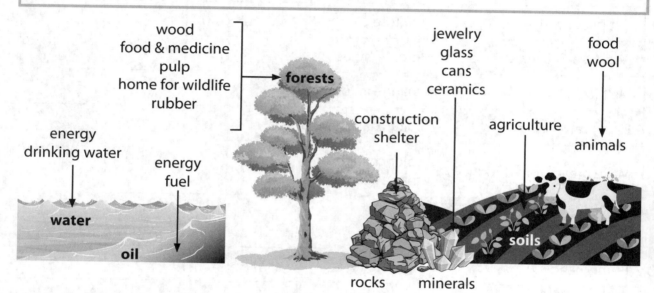

1. All products are made from _____ .

   a. water   **b.** sand

   c. natural resources   **d.** none of the above

2. Plastic is a _____ .

   a. synthetic   **b.** natural resource

   c. system   **d.** glass

3. Both natural and synthetic products are made from natural resources. Why is this a true statement?

   _____

   _____

Physical Science

Name: _____ **Date:** _____

Directions: Read the text, study the chart, and answer the questions.

Aspirin is a pain reliever and heart attack preventer. The key ingredient in aspirin is salicylic acid. It is synthetic. Humans have been using its natural equivalent found in the bark of willow trees for thousands of years. This chart shows other types of products that are available in synthetic and natural forms.

Synthetic	Natural
plastic bag	paper bag
plastic container	glass container
disposable diaper	cloth diaper
polyester, nylon, rayon	cotton, silk, wool fibers
Kevlar	steel
artificial sweetener	sugar
malaria drug Chloroquine	cinchona tree bark
chemotherapy drug Taxol	yew tree bark

1. What is the key ingredient in aspirin?

   a. salicylic acid   **b.** antacid

   c. salt   **d.** none of the above

2. In nature, where is salicylic acid found?

   a. pecan tree   **c.** juniper tree

   b. willow bark tree   **d.** all of the above

3. What question could you ask about a product in the chart?

_____

_____

Analyzing Data

Name: _____ **Date:** _____

Developing Questions

Directions: Read the text, and answer the questions.

Mrs. Lane's class was learning about Kevlar. She said that it is a synthetic fabric. It is made of organic compounds. These are lightweight molecules of carbon, nitrogen, hydrogen and oxygen. Mrs. Lane said that Kevlar is lightweight. It is five times stronger than steel. It protects against bullets, knives, and shrapnel. It is used to make vests, gloves, blast and flame barriers. It is also used in running shoes, bicycle tires, boats, and sails. Kevlar garments have saved the lives of thousands of law enforcement officers.

1. Name two uses of Kevlar.

   a. gloves and vests

   b. bicycle tires and sails

   c. pavement and turf in city parks

   d. both a and b

2. What are the organic properties of Kevlar?

   a. carbon, nitrogen, hydrogen, and oxygen

   b. helium, phosphorous, potassium, and oxygen

   c. magnesium, chlorine, sodium, and hydrogen

   d. nitrogen, magnesium, sodium, and helium

3. Write a question you have about Kevlar.

   _____

   _____

   _____

Name: _____ Date: _____

Directions: Read the text, and answer the questions.

Natural products are made from natural resources, such as wood, sand, trees, and petroleum. A synthetic material is made by chemically changing natural substances to create a new material. A synthetic substance can be chemically identical to a naturally occurring substance, or it can be different.

Reese and Cal were talking. Reese said that when we spend time in the sun, our bodies make Vitamin D naturally. Cal said that we get the same benefit from taking a Vitamin D pill.

"But, that costs money," said Reese, "and natural is always better."

1. What could Cal say to defend his point of view?

   a. Natural products are usually better for the environment.

   b. Taking a vitamin is easier, and more convenient.

   c. Even when it is pouring rain and there is no sunshine, I still get my Vitamin D.

   d. all of the above

2. Which of the following is a renewable resource?

   a. trees

   b. buildings

   c. mountains

   d. soil

3. Which of our natural resources do you think we use the most? Why?

   _____

   _____

   _____

   _____

Planning Solutions

Communicating Results

ABC

Name: _____ **Date:** _____

Directions: Use the word bank to complete the sentences.

aspirin	natural	resources	synthetic
building	paper	sugar	tree
Kevlar	plastic	synthesis	Vitamin D

1. A _____ is a renewable resource.

2. A _____ is not a renewable resource.

3. Both _____ and _____ products are from natural resources.

4. The main ingredient in _____ is salicylic acid.

5. Trees are renewable _____ because they will grow and replenish over time.

6. When we are outside in the sun, our bodies make _____ .

7. _____ is five times stronger than steel.

8. An artificial sweetener is a substitute for _____ .

9. A _____ bag is a substitute for a _____ bag.

10. The process of changing natural resources into synthetic products, such as plastics,

    medicines, and fuels, is called chemical _____ .

Learning Content

Name: _____ Date: _____

Directions: Read the text, and answer the questions.

The Law of Conservation of Mass

We cannot create matter from nothing, and we cannot make matter disappear.

Let's say that you have a capsule. Inside the capsule are five million atoms interacting with one another. Chemical changes are taking place within the capsule, and new substances are being created. But the total number of atoms inside the capsule remains the same. The atoms are not destroyed, and they do not disappear. They still exist in other forms or structures. During a chemical reaction, one substance transforms into another substance of equal mass.

This law helped lay the foundation for modern chemistry. Scientists know that a substance does not disappear, even though it may seem to. The Law of Conservation of Mass was first discovered by Michael Lomonosov and later rediscovered by Antoine Lavoisier in the 18th century.

1. Matter is neither created nor destroyed. It is _____ .

    a. transferred to another planet

    b. transmitted through the airwaves

    c. transformed into another substance of equal mass

    d. none of the above

2. Who discovered the Law of Conservation of Mass?

    a. Isaac Newton

    b. Lomonosov and Lavoisier

    c. Lowell and Lansford

    d. Lemmon and Luke

3. Why do you think it was an important breakthrough for scientists to understand that nothing actually disappears?

    _____

    _____

    _____

Name: _____ **Date:** _____

Analyzing Data

Directions: Read the text, study the chart, and answer the questions.

The atoms that make up an object cannot be created or destroyed. But the atoms can be moved around and changed into different particles. Matter is any substance that has mass and takes up space. It can be weighed on a scale. We cannot make matter out of nothing. We cannot make matter disappear.

What Is Matter? What Is Not?					
Matter	**Not Matter**		**Matter**	**Not Matter**	
water	heat		nitrogen	love	
chair	sunlight		table	reflection	
fork	time		blanket	reflection	
person	idea		paper	gravity	
ice	thought		kitten	energy	
hydrogen	rainbow		pencil	anger	
oxygen	sound				

1. Which one of these is made up of matter?

   a. ice

   b. anger

   c. heat

   d. sound

2. Which one of these is NOT made up of matter?

   a. oxygen

   b. love

   c. fork

   d. chair

3. Why can't we make matter disappear?

   _____

   _____

Name: _____ **Date:** _____

Directions: Read the text, and answer the questions.

Lennie and Jose are working on a science project. The working title of their project is *Energy Is Not Matter*. They are writing their thoughts as they talk about the project. This is what they have written.

A stick of dynamite explodes. Boom. What is happening? A chemical reaction. The chemical energy in the dynamite changes into kinetic energy, heat, and light.

Energy is not matter. Heat and light are not matter. But, energy is carried by atoms. If we could add the atoms of energy created by the explosion, it would equal the original amount of chemical energy in the dynamite. This is called the *conservation of energy*. The energy is kept. It didn't become nothing. It became something else. The number of atoms at the end of the chemical reaction equals the number of atoms when the chemical reaction began.

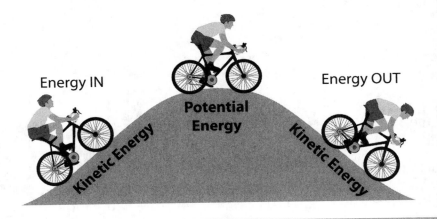

Energy IN   Potential Energy   Energy OUT
Kinetic Energy   Kinetic Energy

1. What is kinetic energy?

   a. the energy that is around us every day

   b. the energy that we use (in) and expend (out)

   c. friction and motion

   d. bicycle wheels

2. If a stick of dynamite explodes, the chemical energy changes into what?

   a. kinetic energy, air mass, and clouds

   b. kinetic energy, heat, and light

   c. kinetic energy and precipitation

   d. physical energy

3. What question would you like to ask about kinetic energy?

_____

_____

Name: _____ Date: _____

Planning Solutions

Directions: Read the text, and answer the questions.

Charles and Olivia are sitting around a fire with Olivia's mom. Charles asks if he can put more coal in the fire since it is cold.

While holding the coal he says he learned in class on Friday that the carbon atom in this piece of coal could be 65 million years old. Olivia agrees and says each atom has a history and how cool that must be. Olivia's mom tells them all atoms that make up living and nonliving things are old but that she is cold so put the coal in the fire.

1. What does every atom have?

   a. a history

   b. nitrogen

   c. oxygen

   d. none of the above

2. How old could the piece of coal have been?

   a. 40 million years old

   b. 65 days old

   c. 20 years old

   d. 65 million years old

3. Describe an atom.

   _____

   _____

   _____

   _____

   _____

Name: _____ **Date:** _____

Directions: Use the word bank to complete the sentences.

Antoine Lavoisier	matter
atoms	products
kinetic energy	sound
mass	The Law of Conservation of Mass

1. The father of modern chemistry is _____.

2. He discovered/proved _____.

3. Reactants transform into _____.

4. The number of _____ at the beginning of a chemical reaction will be the same as at the end.

5. Name one thing that is not matter: _____.

6. The energy that a body possesses because of its motion is called _____.

7. Matter is neither created nor destroyed. It is transformed into another substance of equal

   _____.

8. "Any substance that takes up space and has mass" is the definition of _____.

Learning Content

Name: _____ **Date:** _____

Directions: Read the text, and answer the questions.

Newton's Third Law of Motion

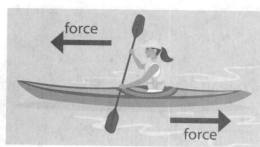

Newton's Third Law of Motion states that for every action, there is an equal and opposite reaction. Let's look at some examples to see what this law means.

- When you paddle a canoe and pull back with the oars, the canoe goes forward.

- When you're swimming, you push the water back with your arms, and your body moves forward.

- When you're standing on a subway train and the train suddenly stops, your body continues to move forward.

- When air rushes out of a balloon, the balloon flies up.

- When you put your hand out of the window in a moving car, the force of the wind pushes your hand back in the opposite direction.

Force is an interaction between one object and another. For example, if you are driving a car at a fast speed and you hit a brick wall the car will come to a stop instantly, but your body will continue moving forward toward the windshield. That is why most cars have airbags and seatbelts to prevent passengers from hitting the windshield, during a collision.

1. "For every action, there is an equal and opposite reaction" describes _____.

   a. something unpleasant and invisible

   b. Newton's Fourth Law of Motion

   c. Newton's Third Law of Motion

   d. Newton's First Law of Motion

2. What is a force?

   a. things that happen when you don't expect them

   b. an interaction between one object and another

   c. a time period between years

   d. none of the above

3. Why do you think Newton's Third Law of Motion is important for rocket scientists to understand?

_____

_____

Name: _____ Date: _____

Directions: Read the text, study the chart, and answer the questions.

> If you push an object, that object pushes back in the opposite direction equally hard. This is another way of saying, "For every action, there is an equal and opposite reaction."

Examples of Newton's Third Law of Motion
rocket blasting off
helicopter taking off
bird flying
person jumping on trampoline
car crashing into tree
diver jumping off diving board at swimming pool
runner at top speed trying to stop instantly

1. Which of the above examples of Newton's Third Law of Motion involves an animal?

    a. car crashing into tree   **b.** person jumping on trampoline

    c. bird flying   **d.** helicopter taking off

2. Which of the above examples of Newton's Third Law of Motion involves space travel?

    a. runner at top speed trying to stop instantly   **b.** rocket blasting off

    c. diver jumping off diving board at swimming pool   **d.** bird flying

3. If you are running at top speed and try to stop suddenly, what happens?

    _____

    _____

    _____

Name: _____ **Date:** _____

Directions: Read the text, and answer the questions.

A pair of figure skaters, Julio and Alyssa, are on the ice. She weighs 135 pounds and is on the shoulders of the man who weighs 195 pounds. They are moving along the ice as one. Julio tosses Alyssa forward through the air and onto the ice. She receives a forward force, and he receives a backward force. The force on Julio is equal to the force on Alyssa. Yet Alyssa's acceleration is greater than Julio's because she is smaller in mass.

We think of a *force* as always causing motion, but a force creates acceleration. Acceleration is an increase in speed. Julio experiences a backward force that causes his backward acceleration. This is also known as deceleration. He slows down while Alyssa speeds up. In every interaction, forces are acting upon both objects.

1. Why is the acceleration of Alyssa greater than the deceleration of Julio?

   a. She is hurrying.

   b. She is smaller in mass.

   c. He is tired from carrying her on his shoulders.

   d. She is a better skater.

2. Why does Julio slow down?

   a. He is injured.

   b. He is ready to quit skating.

   c. He is decelerating backward.

   d. He has lost concentration.

3. Write a question you have about Newton's Third Law of Motion.

_____

_____

_____

Name: _____ **Date:** _____

Directions: Read the text, and answer the questions.

> One day, John was driving. Suddenly, a squirrel ran out onto the road. John swerved to avoid it. His car hit a telephone pole. Of course, John was wearing his seat belt, which kept him from flying forward toward the windshield. His car had been built with a *crumple zone* that absorbed as much of the kinetic energy from the impact as possible. Without the crumple zone, more of the kinetic energy would have been transmitted to John. Luckily, even though the car was damaged, John was fine.

1. What question could you ask about John to verify that he is a good driver?

   a. Do you wear your seatbelt?

   b. Do you drive the speed limit?

   c. Do you watch the road?

   d. all of the above

2. What is another real-life example of Newton's Third Law of Motion?

   a. a baseball being hit by a bat

   b. a stopped car

   c. a ball sitting in the yard

   d. a person sitting in a chair

3. How could the students safely test Newton's Third Law of Motion in the classroom?

   _____

   _____

   _____

   _____

Planning Solutions

Name: _____ Date: _____

Directions: Draw a picture of a toy car crash with two cars hitting one another, head-on. Label them as car A and car B. In a sentence or two, describe what is happening in your picture. These are some words you can use to explain.

collision	impact	speed
energy	Newton's Third Law	thrust
force	of Motion	

_____

_____

_____

_____

© Shell Education

Name: _____ **Date:** _____

Directions: Read the text, and answer the questions.

Balanced Forces

Scientists use several rules, or laws, that explain motion, and the causes of changes in motion. A force must make contact with an object to get it moving or to change its motion. Changes in motion won't just happen on their own. First, let's see what happens when the forces that are acting on an object are balanced.

Imagine two people who both weigh 125 pounds, and they have the same amount of strength. They are standing in a room with a table between them, facing one another. On the count of three, they both start pushing the table in the direction they are facing. Sam is pushing the table toward Dave. Dave is pushing the table toward Sam. What happens to the table? It doesn't move because the forces that are pushing it are balanced, or equal, on both sides.

The rule: A stationary object will not move while the forces acting on it are balanced.

---

1. Forces must act on an object to _____ .

   a. make it stable

   b. get it moving

   c. prepare for a collision

   d. none of the above

2. A stationary object will not move while the forces acting on it are _____ .

   a. weak

   b. secured

   c. balanced

   d. unbalanced

3. Why do scientists study motion?

   _____

   _____

   _____

Analyzing Data

Name: _____ **Date:** _____

Directions: Read the text, study the chart, and answer the questions.

Newton's Second Law of Motion: Acceleration	
Law	**Example**
Acceleration, which is speed or movement, is produced when a force acts on a mass.	A table moves when it is pushed.
The greater the mass of the object being accelerated, the greater the amount of force needed to accelerate the object.	The heavier the table, the harder you have to push.
Force and acceleration are directly proportional.	The harder you push, the faster the object moves.
As the mass of an object is increased, the acceleration of the object is decreased.	If an 80-pound dog jumps up on the table you are moving and takes a nap, the extra weight will slow you down.

1. If you are riding a bicycle and you speed up by pedaling harder, which part of Newton's Second Law of Motion are you applying?

   a. As the mass of an object is increased, the acceleration of the object is decreased.

   b. Acceleration, which is speed or movement, is produced when a force acts on mass.

   c. Force and acceleration are directly proportional.

   d. none of the above

2. If you are riding a bicycle and your younger twin brothers jump on with you, which part of Newton's Second Law of Motion is being applied?

   a. Acceleration, which is speed or movement, is produced when a force acts on mass.

   b. Force and acceleration are directly proportional.

   c. As the mass of an object is increased, the acceleration of the object is decreased.

   d. The greater the mass of the object being accelerated, the greater the amount of force needed to accelerate the object.

3. Which part of Newton's Second Law of Motion is easiest for you to understand?

   _____

   _____

Name: _____ Date: _____

Directions: Read the text, and answer the questions.

> Recall the example of Sam and Dave pushing a table toward one another. The table does not move because the forces acting upon the table are equal, or balanced. The forces are equal because Sam and Dave both weigh 60 kilograms. They both have the same amount of strength.
>
> Larry, who weighs 90 kilograms, walks into the room. He joins Sam on his side of the table, and together, they push the table toward Dave. It is two against one. It's 150 total kilograms against Dave's 60 kilograms. What happens to the table? It moves toward Dave. The forces pushing from the sides of the table are now unbalanced, or unequal.
>
> Newton's Second Law of Motion relates to unbalanced forces acting on an object.

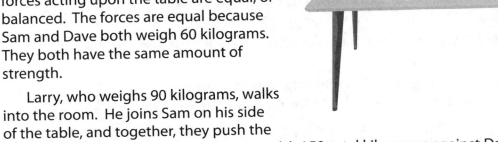

1. When forces are unbalanced, they are _____ .

    a. unequal

    b. unrealistic

    c. undone

    d. unsuccessful

2. Because Dave and Sam weighed the same and had the same strength the force was

    _____ .

    a. heavy

    b. balanced

    c. unbalanced

    d. light

3. What question can you ask about Newton's Second Law of Motion?

_____

_____

_____

Planning Solutions

Name: _____ **Date:** _____

Directions: Read the text, and answer the questions.

On Friday, Mr. Hawkins brought a soccer ball and a bag of marshmallows to class. He weighed the soccer ball at 354 grams. Then he weighed one marshmallow at 7 grams.

He said that mass is the amount of something and it can be measured. A soccer ball has a greater mass than a marshmallow. Everyone understood.

Then he said that acceleration is produced when a force acts on a mass. A soccer ball moves when it is kicked.

Then he said that the greater the mass of the object being accelerated, the greater the amount of force needed to accelerate the object.

On the board, he wrote: It takes more force to kick a soccer ball than to kick a marshmallow. Let's see if this is true.

Mr. Hawkins asked each student to kick the soccer ball and kick the marshmallow. Everyone agreed that Newton was right. It took more force to kick the soccer ball than the marshmallow.

1. What other objects could the children use to test Newton's law?

   a. a basketball and a tennis ball

   b. two bowling balls

   c. a blue pencil and a red pencil

   d. two footballs

2. What will you be measuring in your experiment?

   a. weight

   b. color

   c. force and acceleration

   d. distance

3. Does it seem that Newton's Second Law of Motion is scientific "common sense", meaning that it is easy to understand? Or is it hard to understand? Explain your answer.

   _____

   _____

51412—180 Days of Science

Name: _____ **Date:** _____

Directions: Read the text, and answer the questions.

> Newton wrote a formula to express the concept that Force (F) equals mass (m) multiplied by acceleration (a). The formula is written in this way: $F = ma$. Newton's concepts have been proven over and over again and are used in science, math, physics, and engineering.

1. A car runs out of gas. The gas station is down the street. Bob pushes his car to the station. The car weighs 454 kilograms. Bob is able to push the car one foot per second. Can you identify the mass (m) and the acceleration (a) in this situation?

   a. The car is the mass. The acceleration is one meter per second.

   b. The car is the acceleration. The mass is one meter per second.

   c. The car is the force. The mass is Bob.

   d. Bob is the force. The car is the acceleration.

2. What would help Bob most in this situation?

   a. If the car weighed less.

   b. If the gas station was further away.

   c. If Bob weighed more.

   d. none of the above

3. Write about the way Newton's Laws might be used in any area of science, math, physics, or engineering.

   _____

   _____

   _____

   _____

   _____

   _____

   _____

Communicating Results

Learning Content

Name: _____   **Date:** _____

Directions: Read the text, and answer the questions.

Earth's Magnetic and Geographic Poles

Earth's geographic North Pole is located about 725 kilometers (450 miles) from Greenland. It is called "true north." It is the northernmost point on the Earth. It is in the middle of the icy Arctic Ocean.

Earth also has a magnetic North Pole in northern Canada. It is about 485 kilometers (300 miles) from "true north." The magnetic field extends from Earth's interior into outer space. There the magnetic field meets the damaging solar winds and protects Earth from the sun's charged particles.

When the magnetic field and solar winds collide, the phenomenon called the aurora borealis, occurs. It is also called the "northern lights." The display is seen as streamers of reddish or greenish light in the sky.

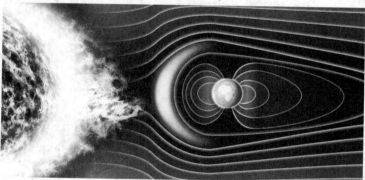

geomagnetic field

magnetic poles

1. Where is Earth's geographic North Pole?

    a. in the icy Arctic Ocean

    c. in North Carolina

    b. in north Alaska

    d. in Canada

2. Where is Earth's magnetic North Pole?

    a. northern Canada

    c. both a and b

    b. about 485 kilometers from "true north"

    d. none of the above

3. What have you learned today that you had never heard before?

    _____

    _____

Name: _____ **Date:** _____

Directions: Read the text, and answer the questions.

Two magnetic items will either attract or repel one another. This is because of the invisible forces of the magnetic field. The northern pole of one magnet is attracted to the southern pole of another magnet.

Compasses use Earth's magnetic field to help people find their way. A compass needle always points to Earth's magnetic South Pole which is near the geographic North Pole.

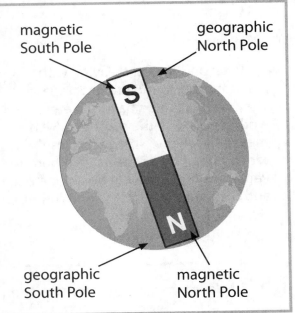

magnetic South Pole

geographic North Pole

geographic South Pole

magnetic North Pole

Analyzing Data

1. When you use a compass, where will the compass needle point?

   a. to the geographic North Pole

   b. to the magnetic South Pole

   c. to the east

   d. to the west

2. All magnets have a _____ .

   a. shift

   b. solar attitude

   c. north and south pole

   d. east and west pole

3. Why do you think the geographic North Pole and the magnetic North Pole are not in the same place?

   _____

   _____

   _____

Developing Questions

Name: _____ **Date:** _____

Directions: Read the text, and answer the questions.

Peter and Nick are playing with magnets they found in the garage. They are picking up nails off Peter's work bench with the magnets. Nick tries to put the two magnets close together, but they repel each other. Peter puts two magnets close together, and they quickly attach to each other.

1. If you place two magnetic items near one another, what will happen?

   a. They will attach and then detach.

   b. They will spin around.

   c. They will either attract or repel one another.

   d. none of the above

2. What will happen if two magnets are attracted to one another?

   a. They will attach to each other in a quick movement.

   b. They will remain static.

   c. They will move in different directions.

   d. They will spin in a circle.

3. What is a question you could ask about magnets or the magnetic field?

   _____

   _____

   _____

   _____

51412—180 Days of Science

© *Shell Education*

Planning Solutions

Name: _____ **Date:** _____

Directions: Read the text, and answer the questions.

Sawyer and Teresa are doing homework together. They are learning that a magnet creates an invisible area of magnetism all around it. This area is called a magnetic field.

They are also learning that it is possible to convert an iron nail into a magnet. This process is called magnetization. It is simple. Take a magnet, and drag it over the nail several times.

1. What is a magnetic field?

    a. an area that is protected

    b. a field that should not be bothered

    c. an invisible area of magnetism

    d. a visible area of magnetism

2. Which household items can you use to recreate the experiment?

    a. plastic bottles

    b. screws

    c. coins

    d. paper

3. What experiment can you do to test which metals are magnetic?

_____

_____

_____

_____

_____

Communicating Results

Name: _____ **Date:** _____

Directions: Read the text. Then, look at the image of the aurora borealis. Write about what is happening in the image.

> The magnetic field protects our planet from the damaging solar winds. When the strong force of the solar winds and the magnetic field meet, colorful streams of reddish and green lights are created. These are called the northern lights or the aurora borealis.

_____

_____

_____

_____

_____

_____

_____

_____

Name: _____ **Date:** _____

Directions: Read the text, study the diagram, and answer the questions.

Kinetic Energy

The word "kinetic" is from the Greek word "kinesis" which means motion. Wind is a good example of kinetic energy because the air moves.

If you have ever ridden a bike uphill, you know that it is hard work. It takes a lot of energy. But, this energy that you are using to go up the hill now will make it easy for you to ride down the hill later. You probably won't even have to pedal. You can coast downhill because you have saved energy. This is potential energy. When you cast down the hill, the potential energy is turned into kinetic energy.

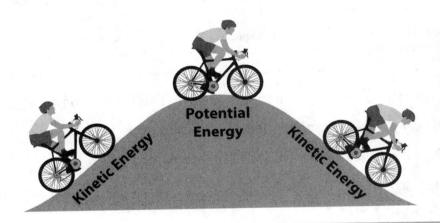

Learning Content

1. What is kinetic energy?

   a. liquid energy

   b. energy in motion

   c. idle energy

   d. transfer energy

2. What is potential energy?

   a. stored energy

   b. the use of energy

   c. the transfer of energy

   d. none of the above

3. What is an example of kinetic energy or potential energy that you have experienced or know about?

_____

_____

_____

Analyzing Data

Name: _____ **Date:** _____

Directions: Read the text, study the diagram, and answer the questions.

Have you ever been on a roller coaster? As the car travels up, it is gaining potential energy. At the top, it has gained the most potential energy. Going down, it gains speed and kinetic energy but loses potential energy. At its highest speed, coming down, the roller coaster has the most kinetic energy and the least stored energy.

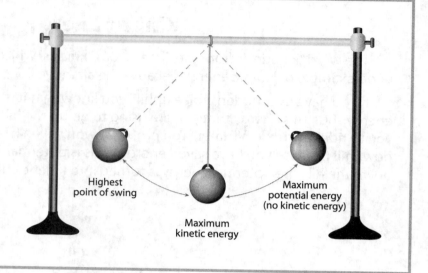

Highest point of swing

Maximum kinetic energy

Maximum potential energy (no kinetic energy)

1. In the roller coaster example mentioned above, when is kinetic energy at its greatest?

   a. when the car is at the top of the ride

   b. when the car reaches its highest speed on the way down

   c. when the ride is over

   d. none of the above

2. When is the stored energy at its greatest?

   a. when the car is at the top of the ride

   b. when the car is at the bottom of the ride

   c. when the ride has ended

   d. before you get on the ride

3. Based on the diagram, where is the ball located when it has the maximum amount of kinetic energy?

   _____

   _____

   _____

   _____

Developing Questions

Name: _____ **Date:** _____

Directions: Read the text, and answer the questions.

> Javier is in the gym on Saturday. He has a basketball, a tennis ball, and his science journal. He wonders whether he can transfer kinetic energy from the basketball to the tennis ball.
>
> First, he bounces the basketball. He records how high it bounces. Then he bounces the tennis ball. He records how high it bounces. Then he holds the tennis ball on top of the basketball and drops them at the same time.
>
> He expects the tennis ball to bounce higher than it did before. He thinks that the basketball will not bounce as high as it did before. He thinks that kinetic energy will transfer from the basketball to the tennis ball.
>
>

1. What does Javier want to find out?

   a. if kinetic energy will transfer from the basketball to the tennis ball

   b. if kinetic energy will transfer from the tennis ball to the basketball

   c. whether stored energy and kinetic energy are the same thing

   d. none of the above

2. What does Javier expect the tennis ball to do when he bounces it the second time?

   a. to bounce higher than it did the first time

   b. to bounce only half as high as it did the first time

   c. to keep bouncing longer than it did the first time

   d. to get in the way of the basketball

3. Write a question you have about transferring energy.

   _____

   _____

Planning Solutions

Name: _____   **Date:** _____

Directions: Read the text, and answer the questions.

Anne's mom is teaching her to play the piano. Anne is lightly touching the keys. Even though her touch is light, her fingers are colliding with the keys for a short time. She is not hurting her fingers or the keys.

When two objects bump into one another this is a collision. This happens when playing the piano, when typing on a keyboard, and even in sports like baseball or soccer.

1. What happens during a collision?

   a. Kinetic energy and potential energy bounce around.

   b. Two objects bump into one another for a short time.

   c. Two objects bump into one another and explode.

   d. none of the above

2. Which is an example of a collision?

   a. two cars traveling side by side on the highway

   b. someone playing a piano

   c. baseball being hit by a batter

   d. both b and c

3. How can you learn more about the transfer of kinetic energy during collisions?

   _____

   _____

   _____

   _____

   _____

Name: _____ **Date:** _____

Directions: Read the sentences. The answer for each blank will be either kinetic or potential. Fill in the blanks with the correct answer.

If a yo-yo is still in your hand, it has _____ energy.

If the yo-yo is moving, it is using _____ energy.

If a bowling ball is being thrown, it is using _____ energy.

If bowling ball is being held, it has _____ energy.

If a rubber band is released, it is using _____ energy.

If a rubber band is being stretched, it has _____ energy.

If a roller coaster at the top of the track, it has _____ energy.

If a roller coaster is rolling down the track, it is using _____ energy.

If an apple is on a limb of the tree, it is using _____ energy.

If the apple is falling from the tree to the ground, it is using _____ energy.

ABC

Communicating Results

Name: _____ Date: _____

Directions: Read the text, and answer the questions.

Static Electricity

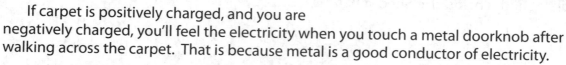

Lightning is a powerful form of static electricity. When a balloon touches your head you experience a mild form of static electricity. Your hair flies in all directions. This is a static charge.

Static electricity is the buildup of an electrical charge on the surface of an object. It happens when the electrical charges of atoms are not moving around. They are all bunched up in one area.

Everything in the world has a positive or negative charge. When one object that has a positive charge touches another object that has a negative charge, electrostatic sparks fly.

If carpet is positively charged, and you are negatively charged, you'll feel the electricity when you touch a metal doorknob after walking across the carpet. That is because metal is a good conductor of electricity.

Lightning is a very powerful example of static electricity. Lightning connects to the ground from the clouds and a second stroke of lightning returns from the ground to the clouds. The heat from the electricity of this return stroke raises the temperature of the surrounding air to around 27,000 °C (48,600 °F).

Sometimes, lightning can be seen from 160 kilometers (100 miles) away. Thunder can be heard from up to 25 kilometers (16 miles) away.

A lightning bolt takes less than one second to split through the air.

1. A static charge is formed when two surfaces touch one another. Why?

   a. Two objects have a positive charge.

   b. Carpets and balloons have strange surfaces.

   c. One object has a positive charge and the other has a negative charge.

   d. none of the above

2. Name a powerful form of static electricity.

   a. carpet

   b. lightning

   c. lightning bug

   d. lamp

3. The buildup of an electrical charge on the surface of an object is called what?

   _____

Name: _____ **Date:** _____

Directions: Read the text, and answer the questions.

Static electricity is the buildup of an electrical charge on the surface of an object. The chart shows you what common materials are least or most likely to cause static electricity.

Materials That Create Static Electricity	
dry hands	more likely
air	
fur	
leather	
glass	
hair	
nylon	
wool	
cotton	
steel	
wood	
nickel	
copper	
silver	less likely

1. What is the least likely to cause static electricity?

   a. wood   **b.** leather

   c. silver   **d.** glass

2. What is most likely to cause static electricity?

   a. dry hands   **b.** cotton

   c. copper   **d.** nylon

3. What material would you use if you wanted to avoid static electricity? Why?

   _____

   _____

   _____

Name: _____ **Date:** _____

Developing Questions

Directions: Read the text, and answer the questions.

Stephanie is watching an oncoming storm from her bedroom window. She sees lightning flash in the distance. She knows that lighting is a powerful form of static electricity. She wonders how close the lightning will get since it can sometimes be seen from 160 kilometers away. She hears thunder too so she knows the storm is close. Thunder can be heard from a distance of 8–25 kilometers.

1. What form of electricity is lightning?

    a. electrical

    b. static

    c. chemical

    d. none of the above

2. In order to hear thunder, how close to it do you have to be?

    a. 80 to 90 kilometers

    b. 2 kilometers

    c. about 8 to 25 kilometers away

    d. about 40 kilometers

3. What is a question you could ask now that you know more about lightning and thunder?

    _____

    _____

Name: _____ **Date:** _____

Directions: Read the text, and answer the questions.

Rachel puts clothes into the dryer. When she gets the clothes out of the dryer, they have static electricity. The reason for the static electricity is lack of moisture. The clothes are overly dry. When clothes are too dry and move around in the dryer, that causes static electricity. To prevent static electricity in the dryer, it can be balanced with dryer sheets.

1. Why do these clothes emit static electricity?

   a. dryer is broken

   b. clothes are overly dry

   c. clothes are too wet

   d. none of the above

2. What could Rachel do to prevent static electricity in her clothes?

   a. balance the static electricity in her dryer

   b. leave the clothes in the dryer longer

   c. take the clothes out of dryer earlier

   d. increase the temperature of the dryer

3. Do research to find out what products reduce static electricity in your dryer. Record your findings.

   _____

   _____

   _____

   _____

Name: _____ **Date:** _____

Directions: Check the box in each row for the material that emits the most static electricity.

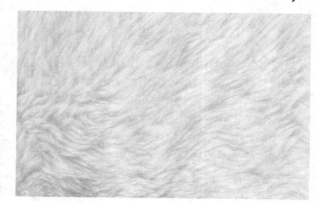

☐ nickel

☐ fur

☐ hands

☐ penny

☐ leather jacket

☐ wood

Learning Content

Name: _____ **Date:** _____

Directions: Read the text, and answer the questions.

Energy is Vital to Life

From energy, we get heat and light. Most of the energy we use comes from fossil fuels. Examples of fossil fuels are petroleum, coal, and natural gas. These took millions of years to form, and someday they will be depleted (gone or almost gone). So, more and more countries are starting to use clean, renewable energy. Renewable energy can come from the sun, wind, water, and even Earth's interior.

Solar power, which is energy from the sun, is a renewable source of energy. The sun's rays can be converted directly to electricity using solar cells. The sun's heat can also be used to create electricity by boiling water. The steam from the boiling water spins a turbine to create electricity.

Heat can be transferred from warmer to cooler areas by conduction, convection, and radiation. Conduction happens when heat flows from the warmer to the cooler object until they are the same temperature. Metal is a good conductor of heat. Convection occurs when warmer areas of a liquid or gas rise to cooler areas. This happens when you boil water. Radiation transfers heat without touching an object directly. For example, we feel heat from the sun, but we are not touching it.

1. Where do we get most of the energy we use?

   a. coal

   b. natural gas

   c. petroleum

   d. all of the above

2. Why are we investing in new technologies for developing energy sources?

   a. We need clean, renewable energy sources.

   b. Someday, fossil fuel energy sources will be gone.

   c. We are planning for the future.

   d. all of the above

3. What are some things we can do to use less energy?

   _____

   _____

Name: _____ Date: _____

Analyzing Data

Directions: Read the text, and study the diagram. Then, answer the questions.

> Conduction, convection, and radiation are the three ways that heat is transferred from warmer to cooler areas.

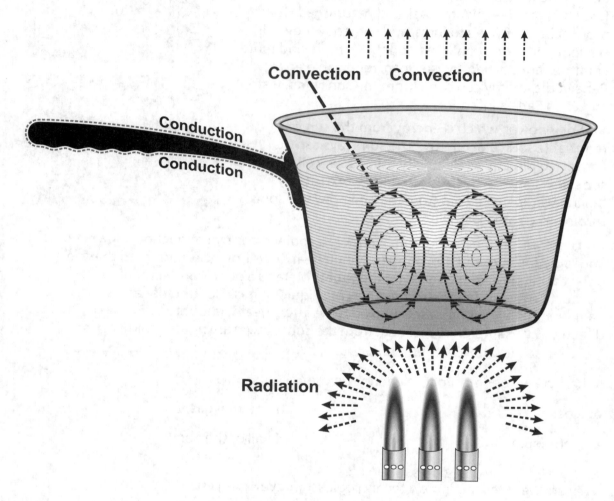

1. Which method of heat transfer is heating up the handle of the pan?

   a. convection

   b. conduction

   c. radiation

   d. all of the above

2. Which method of heat transfer works without the heat source touching the object?

   a. convection

   b. conduction

   c. radiation

   d. all of the above

Name: _____ **Date:** _____

Directions: Read the text, and answer the questions.

> Mona is studying different methods of heat transfer. She has an electric iron, a pot of water, and a stove. She turns on the iron and feels the heat when she puts her hand near it. She puts the pot of water on the stove and turns the heat on. The water begins to boil. The pot is hot.

1. What method of heat transfer is happening when Mona feels the heat from the iron?

   a. radiation

   b. convection

   c. conduction

   d. none of the above

2. What method of heat transfer is happening when the pot gets hot from the stove?

   a. convection

   b. radiation

   c. conduction

   d. none of the above

3. What question can you ask about methods of heat transfer?

   _____

   _____

Developing Questions

Planning Solutions

Name: _____ Date: _____

Directions: Read the text, and answer the questions.

Jorge belongs to a summer camping group. The leader, Mr. Franken, is skilled in many outdoor activities. Last week, he began teaching the group about solar cookers.

Solar cookers convert sunlight to heat energy to cook food. Most cookers have at least one dark-colored surface. Dark colors get very hot in sunlight and absorb more solar radiation than light-colored surfaces. Most solar cookers have reflective panels to direct incoming sunlight toward the dark cooking surface.

1. How do solar cookers work?

   a. They are electric, so you plug them into an outlet.

   b. They convert sunlight to heat energy.

   c. They convert heat energy to sunlight.

   d. They are operated by natural gas.

2. Why might solar cookers be important in undeveloped countries?

   _____

   _____

   _____

3. How could Jorge plan to build his own solar cooker at home?

   _____

   _____

   _____

Name: _____ **Date:** _____

Directions: Use the word bank to answer the questions. Not all of the words will be used.

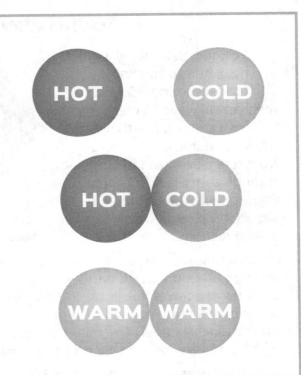

metal
sunlight
heat and light
hotter
heat transfer
convection and radiation
conduction

1. During heat transfer, heat energy flows from _____ temperatures to cooler ones.

2. _____ is a good conductor of heat.

3. The sun provides Earth with huge amounts of energy that can ultimately be used for _____ and _____ .

4. Radiation is a method of _____ that does not rely on contact between the heat source and the heated object.

5. Solar cookers convert _____ to heat energy to cook food.

Communicating Results

Name: _____ **Date:** _____

Directions: Read the text, and answer the questions.

Sound Waves and Energy

We know that sound is what you hear, but do you know what causes sound? Sound is a mechanical wave. A mechanical wave is a disturbance that moves and transports energy from one place to another through a medium, such as air. Sound waves are created by vibrations. Sound waves expand in all directions.

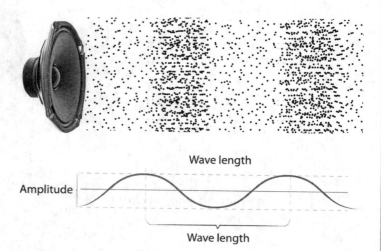

Sound waves can travel through other mediums besides air. They can travel through water or even through solid objects, such as steel. The speed of a sound wave depends on the medium through which it travels. Usually, sound travels faster through solids than through liquids or air.

Sound waves can be described in terms of frequency, pitch, and amplitude. Frequency is how many waves are produced per second. It is measured in hertz (Hz). Pitch is how high or low it sounds. High frequency waves produce high pitch, and low frequency waves produce low pitch. Amplitude determines the loudness of the sound. It is also known as the size of the vibration.

1. What is sound?

   a. a chemical wave

   c. a mechanical wave

   b. a heat wave

   d. a molecule

2. Which is a medium that sound can travel through?

   a. air

   c. water

   b. steel

   d. all of the above

3. How is the speed of sound affected by the medium through which it travels?

   _____

   _____

Name: _____ **Date:** _____

Directions: Read the text, and study the images. Then, answer the questions.

Sound Can Travel Through

gas

liquid

solid

Sound Travels in Waves

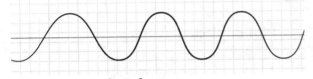

low frequency
few waves per second

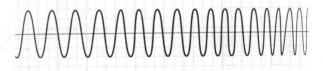

high frequency
many waves per second

1. How does sound travel?

  a. in circles

  b. in waves

  c. in straight lines

  d. none of the above

2. High frequencies are _____ waves per second.

  a. many

  b. few

  c. zero

  d. twenty

3. Sound can travel through _____ .

  a. solids and gas

  b. gas, liquid, and solid

  c. outer space, where there is no air

  d. only air

Analyzing Data

Developing Questions

Name: _____ **Date:** _____

Directions: Read the text, and answer the questions.

Anna is studying for a test in her music class. She uses her voice to practice her pitch.

She is reading about the difference between low pitch sound waves and higher pitch sound waves. She learns that low pitch sound waves have a lower frequency, and high pitch waves have a higher frequency.

lower pitch   higher pitch

1. Higher frequency sound waves have _____ .

   a. more waves per second

   b. fewer waves per second

   c. exactly two waves per second

   d. no waves

2. Does the wave's amplitude affect the pitch of the sound?

   a. Yes, the higher the amplitude, the higher the pitch.

   b. No, the amplitude determines how loud sound is.

   c. Yes, if there is a low amplitude, the pitch is higher.

   d. No, the amplitude is how shrill the sound is.

3. What is a question Anna can ask about sound waves?

   _____

   _____

   _____

Name: _____ **Date:** _____

Directions: Read the directions that Julie followed. Then, in your own words, write what you think she learned.

Julie is conducting an experiment to learn more about sound waves. She has a large metal pan, uncooked rice, and a bowl covered in plastic wrap. She puts a small amount of the rice on top of the plastic wrap. Then she holds the pan near the bowl and bangs on it loudly. The grains of rice jump around on the plastic wrap.

1. What is causing the rice to move?

    a. Sound waves cause the plastic wrap to vibrate.

    b. Julie's hand is creating wind.

    c. The pan is radiating heat.

    d. The rice moves on its own.

2. Do you think the rice would move if Julie just tapped the pan quietly? Why or why not?

    _____

    _____

3. How could Julie change her experiment and get similar results?

    _____

    _____

Communicating Results

Name: _____ **Date:** _____

Directions: Amplitude of a sound wave reflects how loud the sound is. Loudness can be measured in decibels. Study the chart, and graph the data. Then, answer the question.

Sound	Loudness (decibels)
breathing	10 dB
whispering	20 dB
conversation in a quiet area	50 dB
vacuum cleaner	70 dB
blender	88 dB
motorcycle	105 dB
live rock music	110 dB
chain saw	120 dB

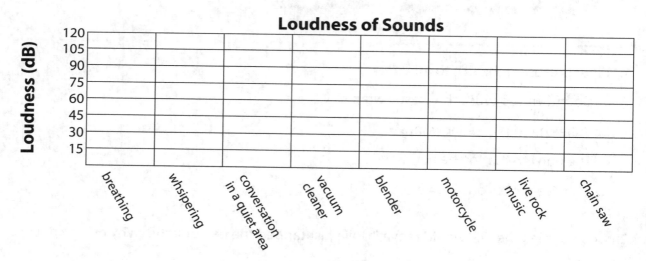

Loudness of Sounds

1. Do you think that sounds can become loud enough to damage your hearing? Why or why not?

_____

_____

Name: _____ **Date:** _____

Directions: Read the text, and answer the questions.

Light Waves

The study of light is called optics. When we talk about "light" we mean light that we can see. Actually, humans can see only a very small part of the entire light spectrum. Notice the slice that is visible to us between the infrared and ultraviolet rays. We can see light within the visible spectrum. The types of waves that we cannot see are radio waves, microwaves, infrared rays, and x-rays.

Light waves can be reflected, absorbed, or transmitted. Reflected means that the light bounces off an object. Absorbed means that the light stops and is taken in by the object. Transmitted means that the light passes through.

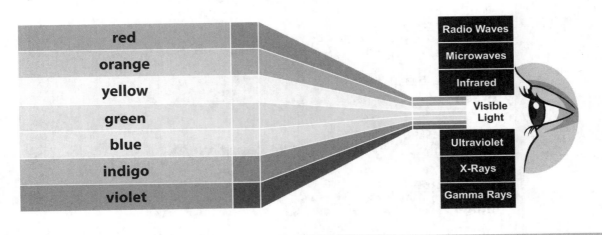

Learning Content

1. Humans can see only a small part of the entire light spectrum. The part that we can see is called what?

   a. the entire spectrum

   b. the light spectrum

   c. the visible spectrum

   d. the color spectrum

2. What are two types of waves that we cannot see?

   a. radio waves and red waves

   b. violet rays and green rays

   c. microwaves and radio waves

   d. ultraviolet waves and red waves

3. What is something you notice about the visible spectrum?

   _____

   _____

Analyzing Data

Name: _____ **Date:** _____

Directions: Read the text, study the diagram, and answer the questions.

> The visible spectrum will always be seen in the same order, whether in a rainbow or a glass prism: red, orange, yellow, green, blue, indigo, violet. Each color in the visible spectrum has a different wavelength. This is the distance between two crests on the wave.

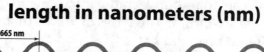

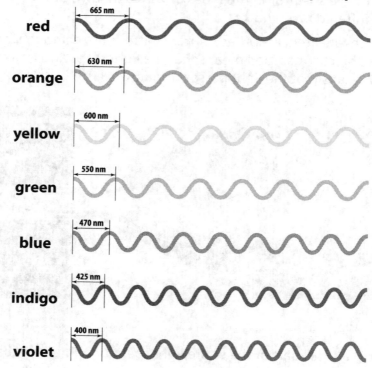

1. Name the colors, in order, that will be seen in a rainbow and a prism.

   a. red, orange, yellow, green, blue, indigo, violet

   b. orange, red, green, blue, violet, indigo

   c. blue, green, yellow, violet, indigo

   d. none of the above

2. Which color has the longest wavelength?

   a. violet

   b. green

   c. red

   d. yellow

Name: _____ Date: _____

Directions: Read the text, study the diagram, and answer the questions.

George and Juan were writing a paper about light waves for science class. They decided to write their paper on reflection, absorption, and transmission. They learned that objects only reflect the color we see. The color of an object is not within the object itself. A red shirt is actually absorbing all the colors of light except red. The red light reflects into our eyes.

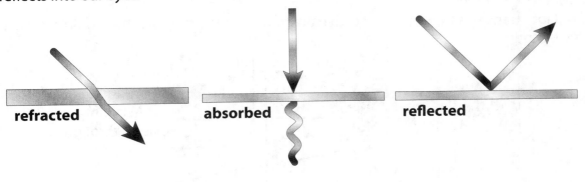

refracted   absorbed   reflected

1. The color of an object is not actually within _____ .

   a. the object itself

   b. the prism

   c. frequency

   d. none of the above

2. When we see an object, we are seeing _____ .

   a. refracted light

   b. absorbed light

   c. reflected light

   d. all of the above

3. What could George and Juan ask about light?

   _____

   _____

   _____

Planning Solutions

Name: _____   **Date:** _____

Directions: Read the text, and answer the questions.

Matt and Nick are in the backyard playing with their flashlights. Nick holds up his flashlight to a glass bottle and then to a piece of tissue paper. The light is transmitted through both of them.

Matt holds his flashlight up to a piece of wood. The light is absorbed by the wood. The wood is opaque.

Light transmits through objects that are translucent and is absorbed by objects that are opaque.

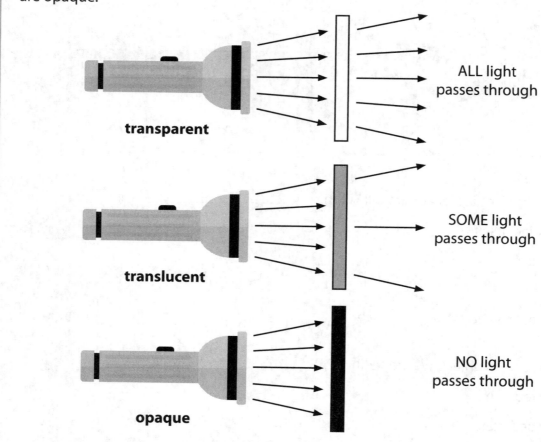

transparent — ALL light passes through

translucent — SOME light passes through

opaque — NO light passes through

1. Light can be transmitted through which types of objects?

   a. transparent or translucent

   b. translucent or opaque

   c. opaque or transparent

   d. any of the above

2. How can Matt and Nick make a model to show what light transmission is?

_____

_____

51412—180 Days of Science

Name: _____ Date: _____

Directions: Use the word bank to complete the sentences.

absorbs	opaque	translucent
black	optics	transparent
crests	reflected	wave
green	reflected	wavelength

1. What color does a green shirt appear to be when the room lights are turned off and the room is entirely dark? _____

2. Wood is _____ . Light cannot travel through it.

3. Clear glass is _____ .

4. Tissue paper is _____ .

5. A light wave can be absorbed, _____ , or transmitted.

6. The wavelength is the distance between two _____ on a wave.

7. When we see an object, we are seeing _____ light.

8. Light is an electromagnetic _____ .

9. We see different colors of light because each color has a different _____ .

10. The study of light is called _____ .

11. A green shirt reflects _____ light and _____ all other colors.

Learning Content

Name: _____ Date: _____

Directions: Read the text, and answer the questions.

The Sun, the Moon, and Earth

Earth orbits the sun, and the moon orbits Earth. The constant motion of Earth and the moon cause many different and amazing things. From Earth, we observe the phases of the moon, solar and lunar eclipses, and seasons. All of these things are the result of the interaction between the sun, Earth, and the moon.

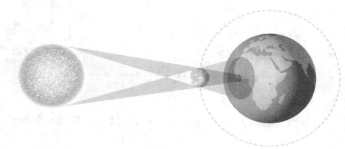

You have likely witnessed the phases of the moon. Each phase is determined by how much of the moon we can see from Earth. The moon does not emit light, but it reflects it from the sun.

An eclipse happens when the sun or moon is temporarily blocked from view. Solar eclipses happen when the moon is between the sun and Earth, which blocks some of the sun's light. A lunar eclipse is when Earth is between the sun and the moon.

Earth is tilted on its axis. As Earth revolves around the sun, parts of Earth are tilted toward the sun and parts are tilted away. This causes the seasons because the part of Earth tilted toward the sun gets more intense sunlight than the parts tilted away.

1. What is a solar eclipse?

   a. When the sun changes its direction.

   b. When the moon moves between the sun and Earth.

   c. When the moon revolves around the Earth.

   d. none of the above

2. What causes Earth's seasons?

   a. lunar eclipses

   b. Earth's rotation

   c. Earth's tilt

   d. the moon

3. What determines the moon's phases?

_____

_____

Name: _____ **Date:** _____

Directions: Read the text, study the diagram, and answer the questions.

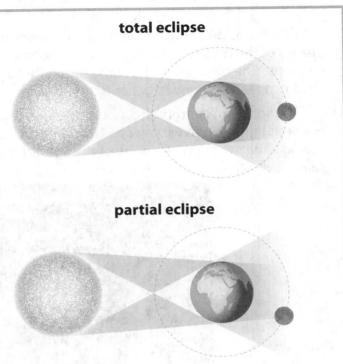

There are two types of lunar eclipses.

A total lunar eclipse occurs when the moon and the sun are on exact opposite sides of Earth.

A partial lunar eclipse happens when only a part of the moon enters Earth's shadow. In a partial eclipse, Earth's shadow appears very dark on the side of the moon facing Earth.

Analyzing Data

1. What are the two types of lunar eclipses?

   a. total and partial

   b. new and waxing

   c. new and waning

   d. half and new

2. What is the position of the moon during a total lunar eclipse?

   a. on the exact opposite side of Earth

   b. next to the sun

   c. in Earth's shadow

   d. none of the above

3. Draw a possible partial lunar eclipse that is different from the diagram above.

Name: _____ **Date:** _____

Directions: Read the text, and answer the questions.

Tiffany has been looking at the moon every night for a month. She observed all the phases of the moon, including the new moon, waxing crescent, full moon, and waning crescent. She took notes about the moon throughout the month and noticed that the moon appears to grow larger and then smaller.

The light we see from the moon is reflected sunlight because the moon itself does not emit light. When we can see 100 percent of the lighted side of the moon, we are seeing a full moon. When none of the lighted side is visible to us, we are seeing what is called a dark moon or a new moon.

1. During which phase of the moon can we see all of the lighted side of the moon?

    a. new moon

    b. full moon

    c. dark moon

    d. waxing crescent

2. If Tiffany watched the moon for another month, what would she observe?

    _____

3. What question can you ask to determine the phase of the moon?

    _____

    _____

Name: _____ **Date:** _____

Directions: Read the text, and answer the questions.

> Roger is studying seasons. He lives in the Northern Hemisphere where it is summer in July. He knows that this is because the Northern Hemisphere is tilted toward the sun during the summer. This means that the sun's rays are more intense on this part of Earth. The Southern Hemisphere is tilted away from the sun in July.
>
>

1. The Southern Hemisphere is experiencing _____ during July.

   a. fall

   b. winter

   c. summer

   d. spring

2. In the Northern Hemisphere, fall comes after summer and before winter. How do you think the sun's rays are affecting Earth during fall?

   _____

   _____

   _____

3. How can Roger make a model of the sun and Earth that would show how Earth's tilt affects the seasons?

   _____

   _____

   _____

Name: _____ **Date:** _____

Directions: Draw a picture to show that you understand the way that Earth's tilt affects the seasons. Label your drawing.

Name: _____ Date: _____

Directions: Read the text, and answer the questions.

Gravity in our Solar System

Gravity is one of the fundamental forces of the universe. It causes every object to attract other objects. It is a powerful force that glues our universe together. It causes the motion of planets, stars, and galaxies. Because of gravity, the moon orbits Earth, and Earth orbits the sun.

Gravity can be defined as the force that pulls two objects toward each other. Anything that has mass also has gravitational pull. The more mass an object has, the stronger its gravitational force. Because Earth's gravitational pull is so strong, we do not notice the pull from other objects. Earth's gravity pulls everything to the center of Earth and prevents us from flying off into space.

Gravity even holds entire galaxies together. Galaxies are stars, gas, and dust held together by gravity. Our solar system is part of the Milky Way galaxy.

Learning Content

1. What is gravity?

   a. the force that draws two objects toward each other

   b. something with glue in it

   c. the force of two things repelling one another

   d. none of the above

2. Gravity is one of the fundamental _____ .

   a. forces of an army

   b. forces of the universe

   c. forces of mankind

   d. forces of black holes

3. Why don't we notice the gravitational pull of objects like books and chairs?

   _____

   _____

   _____

Name: _____ Date: _____

Directions: Read the text, study the diagram, and answer the questions.

Weight is a force caused by gravity. The weight of an object is the gravitational force between the object and Earth. The more mass an object has, the greater its weight. Gravitational force increases when the mass is larger and the object is closer to another object. The images below show animals that weigh what you might weigh on the sun, the moon, and different planets.

If you weighed 45 kg (100 lbs.) on Earth, you'd weigh...

1,218 kg (2,707 lbs.) on the sun

7 kg (17 lbs.) on the moon

17 kg (38 lbs.) on Mercury or Mars

40 kg (91 lbs.) on Venus

113 kg (252 lbs.) on Jupiter

48 kg (106 lbs.) on Saturn

40 kg (89 lbs.) on Uranus

51 kg (113 lbs.) on Neptune

1. If you weighed 45 kg, what would your weight be on the Jupiter?

   a. 113 kg

   b. 40 kg

   c. 51 kg

   d. 91 kg

2. How much would you weight on the moon? The moon only has 1/6 the gravity that Earth does. To know how much you would weigh on the moon, divide your weight by 6.

   _____

Analyzing Data

Name: _____ **Date:** _____

Directions: Read the text, study the diagram, and answer the questions.

Jenna learned that every object in the universe that has mass exerts a gravitational pull on every other mass. She is making a model to represent how gravity holds the moon in Earth's orbit. She holds a string attached to a tennis ball and spins around. When she lets go of the string, the ball flies off in a straight line in the direction it was going when she let go.

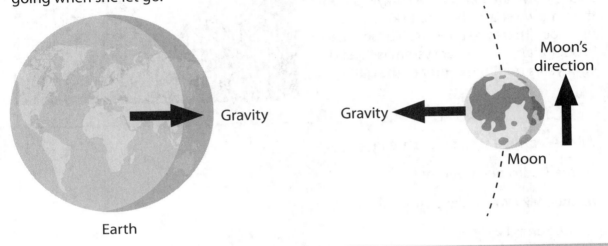

Earth

Gravity

Gravity

Moon's direction

Moon

Developing Questions

1. Without Earth's gravity, what would happen to the moon?

_____

_____

_____

2. Every object in the universe that has _____ exerts a gravitational pull.

3. What is a question you have about gravity's effect on you?

_____

_____

4. What is a question you have about gravity's effect on the solar system?

_____

_____

_____

Planning Solutions

Name: _____ **Date:** _____

Directions: Read the text, and answer the questions.

> Gavin is reading a book about the Milky Way Galaxy. He learns that Earth, the sun, and all the other planets in our solar system are part of the Milky Way. All the stars we see in the night sky are part of it, too. There are about 100 billion stars in our galaxy. Our solar system is 25,000 light years from the center of the galaxy.

1. All the stars we see at night are in _____ .

   a. the Andromeda Galaxy

   b. the Milky Way Galaxy

   c. the Series I Galaxy

   d. the Earth Galaxy

2. How could Gavin create a model of the Milky Way, and where should he place our solar system within it?

   _____

   _____

   _____

3. Within our solar system, what are two or three "objects" that circle around other things? For example: the moon circles around the _____ .

   _____

   _____

   _____

Name: _____ **Date:** _____

Directions: Study the chart, and graph the data. Then, answer the question.

Location	Mass (kg)
Earth	42
the moon	7
Mercury	16
Venus	38
Mars	16
Jupiter	106
Saturn	45
Uranus	37
Neptune	47

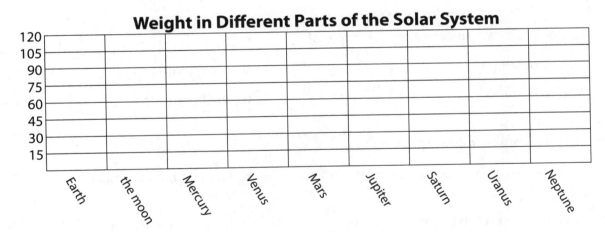

Weight in Different Parts of the Solar System

1. What would jumping on Jupiter be like compared to jumping on the moon? How do you know?

_____

_____

© Shell Education

51412—180 Days of Science

143

Communicating Results

Learning Content

Name: _____ **Date:** _____

Directions: Read the text, and answer the questions.

Objects in the Solar System

The universe is all of space and time. Its contents include planets, moons, stars, and galaxies. It also includes the contents of intergalactic space and all matter and energy. While the size of the entire universe is still unknown, it is possible to measure the observable universe.

When we think about how large the universe must be, our own solar system can seem small by comparison. Our solar system consists of the sun and all of the objects orbiting it. These objects are planets, moons, asteroids, dwarf planets, comets, gas, and dust. A planet is a large space object that revolves around a star. Some of the planets in our solar system, including Earth, are made of rock. Some are made of gas. Earth is one of eight planets orbiting the sun.

Our sun is a star. It is also the largest object in our solar system. Ninety-eight percent of all matter in the solar system is found within the sun. Our sun is not unique in the universe. There are trillions of other stars in the universe just like it. Many of these stars have their own systems of planets.

Our sun is a common, middle-sized, yellow star that scientists have named Sol, after the ancient name given to it by the Romans. That is why our system of planets is called the solar system.

1. Planets in our solar system are made of _____ .

   a. dust or gas

   b. rock or dust

   c. rock or gas

   d. dust or energy

2. Which of the following is true?

   a. Our sun is the same size as the moon.

   b. Our sun is a common, medium-sized yellow star.

   c. Our sun is the largest star in the universe.

   d. none of the above

3. What kind of discoveries do you think might be made as scientists continue to study our solar system?

_____

_____

_____

Name: _____ Date: _____

Directions: The sun is at the center of our solar system. The chart shows the order of the planets, starting with the closest planet to the sun. Study the chart, and answer the questions.

Planet	Order from the Sun	Terrestrial or Gas?
Mercury	1	terrestrial
Earth	2	terrestrial
Venus	3	terrestrial
Mars	4	terrestrial
Jupiter	5	gas
Saturn	6	gas
Uranus	7	gas
Neptune	8	gas

Analyzing Data

1. Which planet is closet to the Sun?

   a. Neptune   **b.** Mercury

   c. Mars   **d.** Earth

2. Which is the closest gas planet?

   a. Mercury   **b.** Mars

   c. Jupiter   **d.** Neptune

3. Which planet do you think takes the longest to orbit the sun? Why?

   _____

   _____

   _____

   _____

Developing Questions

Name: _____   Date: _____

Directions: Read the text, study the diagram, and answer the questions.

Jeff is studying the orbit of the planets around the sun. The planets in our solar system are held in place by gravity. Each planet has its own individual orbit, so each planet's year differs. Below is a diagram that Jeff made showing how long different planets take to complete one orbit around the sun. The numbers are in Earth days and years.

Time for the Planets to Complete One Orbit Around the Sun

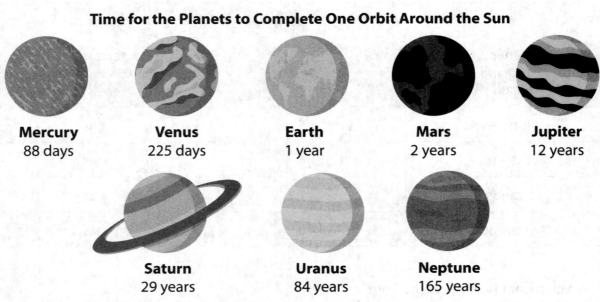

| **Mercury** | **Venus** | **Earth** | **Mars** | **Jupiter** |
| 88 days | 225 days | 1 year | 2 years | 12 years |

| **Saturn** | **Uranus** | **Neptune** |
| 29 years | 84 years | 165 years |

1. Which planet takes the shortest amount of time to orbit the sun?

   a. Saturn   **b.** Uranus

   c. Mercury   **d.** Jupiter

2. What planet takes two years to orbit the sun?

   a. Mercury   **b.** Mars

   c. Saturn   **d.** Pluto

3. What question could you ask about the time it takes for a planet to orbit the sun?

   _____

   _____

   _____

Name: _____ Date: _____

Directions: Read the text, and answer the questions.

> Delilah is studying the solar system. She learns that there are many objects in our solar system that are not planets. Dwarf planets are objects that orbit the sun but do not meet the criteria to be considered a planet. Pluto, which is farther from the sun than Neptune, used to be considered a planet, but it was demoted to dwarf planet status in 2006. The other dwarf planets in our solar system are Ceres, Haumea, Makemake, and Eris.

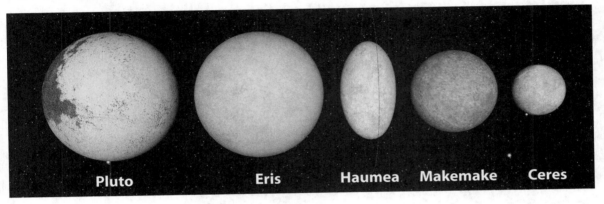

1. Why isn't Pluto considered a planet?

   a. It doesn't orbit the sun.

   b. It doesn't meet the criteria.

   c. It is the moon of Neptune.

   d. It is an asteroid.

2. Where is Pluto located related to the planets?

   a. after Jupiter and before Saturn

   b. after Mercury and before Venus

   c. after Neptune

   d. before Neptune

3. How could Delilah build a model of the solar system that would include Pluto and the other dwarf planets?

   _____

   _____

   _____

   _____

   _____

Planning Solutions

Name: _____ **Date:** _____

Directions: Label the planets of our solar system, and answer the question.

Earth	Mercury	Uranus
Jupiter	Neptune	Venus
Mars	Saturn	

1. What other objects are located in our solar systems besides planets?

_____

_____

_____

_____

_____

Communicating Results

Name: _____ **Date:** _____

Directions: Read the text, and answer the questions.

Learning Earth's History

Layers of rock are called *strata*. Scientists study the strata as a way to understand Earth's 4.6-billion-year history. Each layer can give insight into the past. They can tell us what types of plants and animals lived during different time periods.

Throughout time, layer after layer of sediment was deposited. This means that rock layers form from the bottom up. The newest layers are on top, and the oldest layers are on the bottom. Understanding this is fundamental to studying Earth's history. In any area where sedimentary rock is found, there are clues to the relative ages of the rock layers and the fossils.

Learning Content

1. What are rock layers called?

   a. particle

   b. composition

   c. strata

   d. fossil

2. What must you understand to study Earth's history?

   a. that a rock bed must be a particular color

   b. that a rock bed must be older than any layer on top of it

   c. that a rock bed must have fossils

   d. none of the above

3. What are some things you can learn from studying different rock layers?

   _____

   _____

   _____

Analyzing Data

Name: _____ **Date:** _____

Directions: Read the text, study the diagram, and answer the questions.

Most fossils are found in sedimentary rock. Fossils are the remains of prehistoric plants and animals that have been preserved in rock. They offer a great deal of information about the time periods of Earth's history.

Time 1: A layer of sediment is deposited into a lake horizontally.

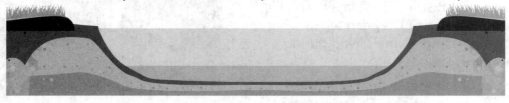

Time 2: Later in time, a second layer is deposited on top of the first.

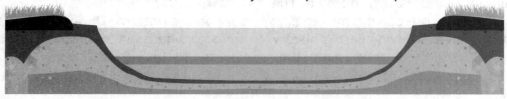

Time 3: Even later in time, a third layer is deposited on top of the first two.

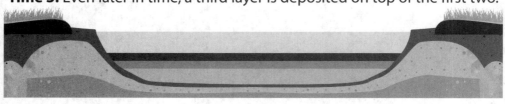

1. In what type of rock are most fossils found?

   a. igneous

   b. sedimentary

   c. metamorphic

   d. volcanic

2. Where is the oldest layer of rock found?

   a. top

   b. middle

   c. bottom

   d. none of the above

3. How do you think scientists use rocks to study the history of Earth?

   _____

   _____

   _____

Name: _____ Date: _____

Directions: Read the text, and study the diagram. Then, answer the questions.

Rafi is a scientist who is studying a fossil. He knows his fossil is a flowering plant fossil from the Mesozoic Era. He is trying to determine which time period the fossil is from. He is using information he has about the Mesozoic Era to figure out a relative age for his fossil.

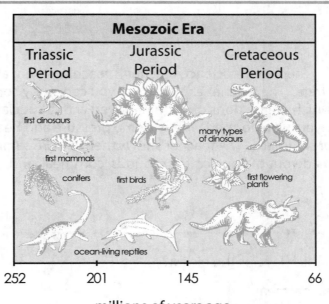

Mesozoic Era

Triassic Period | Jurassic Period | Cretaceous Period

first dinosaurs

first mammals

conifers   first birds

many types of dinosaurs

first flowering plants

ocean-living reptiles

252   201   145   66

millions of years ago

Developing Questions

1. The fossil must be _____ years old or newer.

   a. 66 million

   b. 6 million

   c. 145 million

   d. 14 million

2. Would it be possible to find a bird fossil in a rock layer that was 250 million years old? Why or why not?

   _____

   _____

   _____

3. What is a question you might ask about geological time in relationship to layers of Earth?

   _____

   _____

   _____

Name: _____ **Date:** _____

Directions: Read the text, and answer the questions.

Stephanie's science teacher is teaching them about rock strata. The teacher explains that you can study core samples, which are sections of Earth removed with a special drill. The layers were formed with extreme pressure and heat, magma, or sediment. The teacher shows them a "core sample" that she made out of flour, coffee grounds, cornmeal, and oatmeal.

oatmeal
cornmeal
coffee grounds
flour

1. Which layer is the oldest?

   a. oatmeal

   b. cornmeal

   c. coffee grounds

   d. flour

2. If the coffee layer is 250 billion years old, how old could the flour layer be?

   a. 200 billion years old

   b. 100 billion years old

   c. 230 billion years old

   d. 300 billion years old

3. Describe how you could make your own core sample model and what the different parts would be.

   _____

   _____

   _____

   _____

Name: _____ **Date:** _____

Directions: Draw layers of sedimentary rock. Label the oldest and newest layers. Then, answer the questions.

1. Describe the layers of your sedimentary rock.

   _____

   _____

2. How do strata help scientists discover the exact age or the relative age of Earth's layers?

   _____

   _____

   _____

Name: _____ Date: _____

Learning Content

Directions: Read the text, and answer the questions.

Changes in Earth's Surface

Earth's surface is constantly changing. Changes can occur over long periods of time. They can also be quick and severe. Two great forces that change Earth's surface are erosion and weathering. Erosion is when Earth's surface is worn away and bits of rock or soil are carried away and deposited elsewhere. Moving water, wind, and ice can all cause erosion.

Weathering is similar to erosion, but during weathering, debris is not carried away. Weathering is the breakdown or change of Earth's surface due to weather conditions. It occurs mainly though the effects of wind, water, and temperature on rocks and soil. Weathering and erosion often occur together. The weathering of rock is a slow, ongoing process.

1. What are two great forces that change Earth's surface?

   a. rain and snow

   c. weathering and erosion

   b. temperature and rain

   d. snow and hail

2. The breaking down of rock, due to weathering, is _____ .

   a. a misunderstood process

   c. a quick and easy process

   b. a slow and ongoing process

   d. none of the above

3. What is the main difference between weathering and erosion?

   _____

   _____

   _____

Name: _____ **Date:** _____

Directions: Study the chart. Then, answer the questions.

Event	Effect
moving water	Moving water slowly wears down rock surfaces. Loose particles of rock or soil are carried away and deposited elsewhere.
temperature change	When air temperature changes greatly over a few hours, rocks can expand, contract, and rupture.
transportation and sedimentation	Materials eroded by wind or water are carried away and deposited at lower elevations. These new deposits can later turn into rocks.
freezing water	When water freezes inside tiny holes or fissures in rocks, they expand and shatter.

1. When the air temperature changes greatly over a short period of time what happens to rocks?

   a. They expand, contract, and rupture.

   b. They remain stagnant.

   c. They melt.

   d. They change colors.

2. When water penetrates into rock fissures, what happens to the rocks?

   a. They explode and regenerate.

   b. They expand and shatter.

   c. They roll away.

   d. none of the above

3. Why do you think scientists study changes to Earth's crust?

   _____

   _____

Analyzing Data

Developing Questions

Name: _____   **Date:** _____

Directions: Read the text, and answer the questions.

Brittney is exploring a large rock at a nearby park. The rock has large cracks in it, and she notices that there are some pieces that have broken off. It rained earlier that day, and the temperatures will get below freezing that night. She is wondering how the freeze-thaw cycle will affect the rock.

magma   **metamorphic rock**

1. What type of weathering will happen as a result of the weather described?

   a. wind

   b. water

   c. freeze-thaw

   d. rock

2. Would this type of weathering occur over a long or short period of time? How do you know?

   _____

   _____

   _____

3. What is a question you could ask about weathering?

   _____

   _____

   _____

Earth and Space Science

Planning Solutions

Name: _____   **Date:** _____

Directions: Read the text, and answer the questions.

William is visiting Arches National Park in Utah. This park is an example of how wind erosion can shape rock into different formations. The arches took millions of years to form. They were created as a result of erosion from wind, water, and ice. William wants to learn more about the rock formations in the park.

1. Is erosion still affecting the arches?

   a. No, the erosion stopped many years ago.

   b. Yes, erosion will happen as long as there is wind and moving water.

   c. No, rock formations stop eroding after a certain point.

   d. Yes, but now the erosion is caused by animals.

2. How many years did it take for the arches to form?

   a. thousands of years

   b. hundreds of years

   c. millions of years

   d. ten years

3. How could William create a model to simulate wind erosion?

   _____

   _____

   _____

   _____

   _____

Name: _____ **Date:** _____

Directions: Draw something before and after erosion. Then, answer the question.

Communicating Results

Before
After

1. Explain your two drawings. What kind of erosion caused the changes?

_____

_____

_____

Name: _____ **Date:** _____

Directions: Read the text, and answer the question.

Continental Drift

The rigid, rocky, outer layer of Earth includes Earth's crust and the upper part of the mantle. Scientists believe that many years ago, all the continents were joined together as one gigantic continent called *Pangaea*. A slow and constant movement over millions of years broke the outer layer of Earth in many places. This divided the crust into tectonic plates. This movement is called *continental drift*. Seafloor spreading is part of continental drift. It happens at the bottom of an ocean as tectonic plates move apart and carry continents with them. This is how Pangea transformed from one continent to seven.

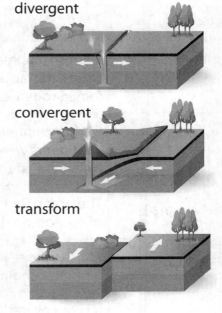

divergent

convergent

transform

Deep in the earth, heat from the core rose through the mantle to the surface. The heat moved the mantle, which rose beneath the earth's crust before spreading sideways and cooling. Once the mantle cooled, it sank again. In some places, the plates pulled apart, and new crust was pushed up from below. These areas were called divergent boundaries, creating rifts or valleys. In other places, the plates pushed against each other, creating mountains that were known as convergent boundaries. Transform boundaries occurred when plates slid past one another but did not collide or rip apart. The San Andreas Fault in California is a transform boundary.

1. When plates push against each other, creating mountains, these are called _____ .

   a. valleys

   b. hills

   c. convergent boundaries

   d. divergent boundaries

2. The San Andreas Fault in California is a _____ .

   a. mountain

   b. transform boundary

   c. drift

   d. valley

3. Why do scientists study tectonic plates?

   _____

   _____

Learning Content

Name: _____ **Date:** _____

Analyzing Data

Directions: Modern theories of continental drift took many years to form. Study the chart, and answer the questions.

Year	Event
1596	Flemish mapmaker Abraham Ortelius observed that coastlines of the continents appear to fit together. He thought continents were once joined together.
1912	German meteorologist and geophysicist Alfred Wegener suggested that continents were once joined together into one continent called Pangea. He proposed the theory of continental drift.
1950s	The ocean floor was mapped and provided data leading to the discovery of mid-ocean ridges.
1960	The idea of seafloor spreading is developed. The modern theory of plate tectonics begins to form.
mid-1960s	It is discovered that earthquakes and volcanic activity occur frequently at the edges of tectonic plates.
1968	Core samples from a mid-ocean ridge reveals that rocks close to mid-ocean ridges are younger than those farther away from the ridges.

1. How long ago did someone first theorize that the continents were once joined together?

  a. over 400 years ago
  b. about 50 years ago
  c. about 100 years ago
  d. about 20 years ago

2. After the theory of continental drift was proposed, how long did it take to figure out what causes it?

  a. 8 years
  b. 27 years
  c. 20 years
  d. 400 years

3. Do you think that the theory of continental drift will continue to change? Why or why not?

  _____

  _____

Name: _____ Date: _____

Directions: Read the text, study the diagram, and answer the questions.

> Mrs. Keller's class is reading about seafloor spreading. It is part of the theory of plate tectonics. It happens at the bottom of an ocean as tectonic plates move apart. The seafloor moves and carries continents with it. At ridges in the middles of oceans, material from the mantle is pushed upward, forcing the crust apart, and causing continental drift.

1. What is seafloor spreading?

    a. As tectonic plates dissolve, the seafloor moves.

    b. As tectonic plates move apart, the seafloor moves and carries continents with it.

    c. As the seafloor moves, tectonic plates are nearby.

    d. none of the above

2. Seafloor spreading is related to what theory?

    a. plants

    b. planets

    c. plate tectonics

    d. platelets

3. What questions do you have about the ocean floor?

    _____

    _____

Planning Solutions

Name: _____ **Date:** _____

Directions: Read the text, and answer the questions.

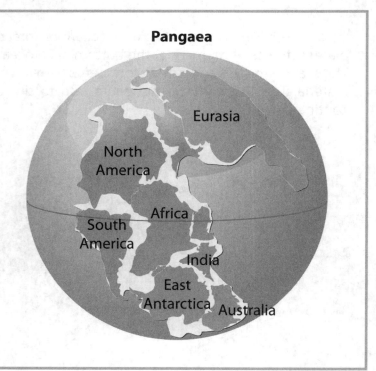

Pangaea

Jenna is learning about how continental drift affected the location of fossils. It appears that continental drift moved fossil remains. Scientists believe that during the time of Pangaea, living things were able to move about freely. But, the breaking of the continent separated them from their original homes. In addition to fossils, geologists have also found glacial scars. This indicates that the fossils were made in one location, along with the glaciers, and were then separated by great distances.

1. Would it be possible to find fossils from the same animal on more than one continent?

   a. Yes, because of continental drift.

   b. No, all animals only lived on one continent.

   c. Yes, because people moved the fossils.

   d. No, fossils do not exist.

2. What indicates that fossils were made in one location and then separated by great distances?

   a. fossil remains

   b. Pangea

   c. glacial scars

   d. continent scars

3. How could Jenna learn more about Pangaea and continental drift?

   _____

   _____

   _____

Name: _____ Date: _____

Directions: Write a story about a dinosaur who was living in Pangaea. Then, Pangaea broke apart. Include details about how the crust changed and how it affected the dinosaur.

Millions and millions of years ago… _____

_____

_____

_____

_____

_____

_____

_____

_____

_____

_____

_____

_____

_____

_____

_____

_____

_____

_____

_____

_____

_____

Communicating Results

ABC

Learning Content

Name: _____ Date: _____

Directions: Read the text, and answer the questions.

Cycles of Matter and Energy on Earth

Let's look at three words, and what they mean, in relation to the cycles of matter and energy on Earth.

1. Producers are green, living plants. Through the process of photosynthesis, producers use energy from the Sun to produce food.

Post oak trees are producers.

The post oak tree is a **producer**.

2. Consumers are living organisms that cannot make their own food. They feed on producers or other consumers to survive. All animals are consumers. Bears are consumers. They will eat almost anything, including rabbits, skunks, berries, nuts, and bugs.

Deer only consume plants.

Deer are **consumers** that eat only plants.

3. Decomposers feed on dead organisms or the waste of living organisms. They take dead animals and plants, and break them down into individual nutrients in the soil. Then, they are re-used by plants to make more food. Fungus grows on the sides of trees, and slowly decomposes it.

Beetles and bugs are considered decomposers since they feed on dead organisms.

Beetles and bugs are **decomposers**.

1. What are producers?

   a. bugs   **b.** deer

   c. green, living plants   **d.** rabbits

2. What are consumers dependent on for survival?

   a. producers or other consumers   **b.** dirt

   c. fur   **d.** none of the above

3. What would happen if all of the producers on Earth died?

_____

_____

51412—180 Days of Science

Name: _____ **Date:** _____

Directions: Read the text, and answer the questions.

> Decomposers and scavengers are valuable to our Earth. Decomposers break down waste and dead organisms, and return the raw materials to the dirt. There, they are "recycled" into the ecosystem. Scavengers take whatever is left after the decomposers have done their work. Scavengers eat the dead remains of organisms that no other organism will eat; decaying meat or rotting plant material. Hyenas, vultures, catfish, jackals, crows, and roaches are scavengers.
>
> Hyenas have extremely strong jaws that are adapted to crush animal bone. The California condor, a type of vulture, is one of the largest North American birds of prey.

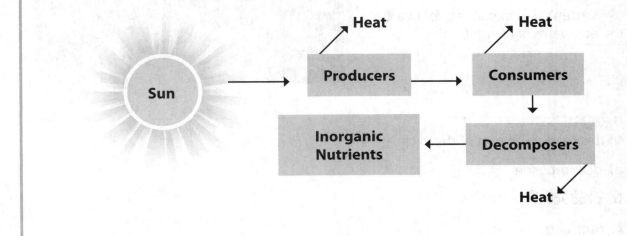

1. In what order does energy flow, in the ecosystem?

   a. from consumers to decomposers to producers

   b. from producers to consumers to decomposers

   c. from decomposers to producers to consumers

   d. none of the above

2. What does a consumer do?

   a. makes certain that no animals in the forest are safe

   b. feeds on producers or other consumers

   c. carries off living organisms and buries them in forests

   d. do not eat

3. If you came across a decomposer in the forest, what might it be doing?

   _____

   _____

Name: _____ Date: _____

Directions: Read the text, and answer the questions.

Developing Questions

Kristen and her family are on a camping trip. They decide to go for a hike to the lake. Next to the lake they find a dead fish. The fish has started to decompose. It has some worms on it and has been sitting in the sun.

Kristen's dad explains this is part of the ecosytem of life on Earth.

1. In this case, what part of the cycle are the worms?

   a. decomposers

   b. producers

   c. nutrients

   d. consumers

2. What type of energy is the Earth receiving from the fish?

   a. heat

   b. water

   c. bones

   d. none

3. What is another question that Kristen could ask her dad about this process?

   _____

   _____

   _____

   _____

Name: _____ **Date:** _____

Directions: Study the diagrams. Then, plan an experiment of your own that re-creates the movement of carbon through a plant.

The Carbon Cycle

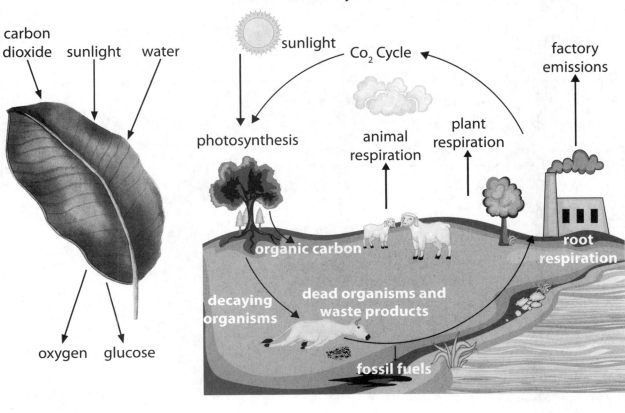

Planning Solutions

_____

_____

_____

_____

_____

_____

_____

_____

_____

_____

Name: _____ **Date:** _____

Directions: Write whether each living thing in the chart is a producer, consumer, or decomposer.

worm	
peach tree	
lion	
apple tree	
cabbage	
robin	
catfish	
deer	
fungus	

Name: _____ **Date:** _____

Directions: Read the text, and answer the questions.

Weathering

Weathering is a natural process that happens over time. It causes rocks to break down. The three types of weathering are chemical, physical, and biological.

Chemical weathering decays rocks and minerals. This occurs when rocks interact with chemicals such as oxygen, carbon dioxide, water, and acids. When this happens, rocks break down or change color. This often takes place in caves.

Physical weathering breaks rocks into smaller pieces. This happens naturally because of heat from the sun, running water, or shifting ice. With physical weathering, no chemical changes occur. An example of physical weathering is frost action or shattering. This happens when water gets into cracks in bedrock. As the water freezes, it expands, and the cracks are opened a little wider.

Biological weathering can be caused by bacteria or fungi, and by plants that break down rocks with their roots.

1. What is chemical weathering?

   a. bedrock

   b. frostbite of rocks

   c. decay of rocks

   d. lack of rocks

2. What is physical weathering?

   a. wide openings in minerals

   b. the breakup of rock without chemical changes

   c. physical hardships

   d. none of the above

3. Why do scientists study weathering?

_____

_____

Learning Content

Analyzing Data

Name: _____ Date: _____

Directions: Study the infographic. Then, answer the questions.

Weathering
Weathering causes rock to break down. Weathering happens before erosion does. Weathering does not involve movement of the broken rock.

Erosion
Erosion always involves movement in a downhill direction.

Deposition
When sediment is dropped in a location, time after time, the buildup changes the landscape. Deposition creates sand dunes in the desert, and sandy beaches near the ocean.

1. In what direction does erosion always occur?

    a. downhill   **b.** uphill

    c. south   **d.** west

2. Erosion always involves _____.

    a. dedication   **b.** justification

    c. pace   **d.** movement

3. Why is the Earth's surface constantly changing?

_____

_____

_____

Name: _____ Date: _____

Directions: Read the text, and answer the questions.

> Emily spent time with her brother learning about the sand and the surf when he was home on vacation. They liked to walk on the sandy beaches. Emily's brother was helping her learn about weathering and erosion for school. On the beach he showed her how it happened.

1. How did the sand on the beach get there?

   a. by rail car

   b. by deposition

   c. by erosion

   d. by weathering

2. What are four natural causes of weathering, erosion, and deposition?

   a. animals, water, weeds, and wind

   b. seeds, wind, hail, and copper

   c. wind, water, ice, and gravity

   d. none of the above

3. _____ is the process by which sediment is deposited in a new location.

   a. Deposition

   b. Erosion

   c. Weathering

   d. Winter

4. What question could you ask about the processes of weathering, erosion, and deposition on the beach?

   _____

   _____

Developing Questions

Planning Solutions

Name: _____ **Date:** _____

Directions: Read the text, write a plan for Kim to record and analyze the results of her experiment.

> Kim is doing an experiment on weathering. She puts 5 M&M's on a tin pan. Each day for a week she uses a pipet to place 6 drops of water on the first M&M, 5 drops on the second, 4 drops on the third and so on. She wants to study how water (rain) will affect the structure and the color of the M&Ms.

_____

_____

_____

_____

_____

_____

_____

_____

_____

_____

_____

_____

_____

_____

_____

_____

_____

_____

Name: _____ **Date:** _____

Directions: Label the processes of weathering, erosion, and deposition.

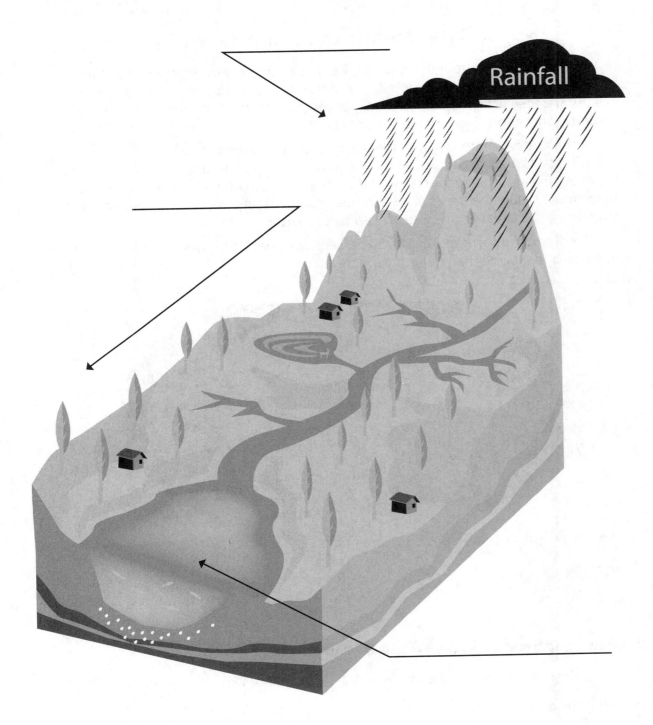

Learning Content

Name: _____ **Date:** _____

Directions: Read the text, and answer the questions.

The Oceans of Planet Earth

Seventy one percent of the water on Earth is in our oceans. Our planet has five great oceans, and they are all joined. In order of size, from largest to smallest, the oceans are: the Pacific; Atlantic; Indian; Southern (Antarctic); and Arctic. Scientists have explored only about five percent of our oceans.

At the bottom of the ocean is the ocean floor. Deep below the surface of the water are mountains, plains, volcanoes, and trenches. This is an underwater world, filled with living organisms. The deepest part of the ocean is the Mariana Trench. It is located seven miles below the ocean waves, in the western Pacific Ocean. The largest living structure is the Great Barrier Reef. It can be seen from the moon.

The ocean produces more than 50 percent of the world's oxygen. It stores 50 times more carbon dioxide than our atmosphere.

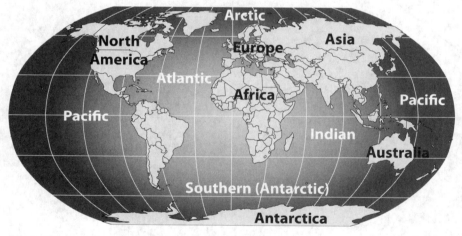

1. How many great oceans does our planet have?

   a. 3

   c. 2

   b. 8

   d. 5

2. What is important about the Mariana Trench?

   a. It is the deepest part of the ocean.

   c. It is full of carbon.

   b. It is a place where treasure is hidden.

   d. It is a secret.

3. Why do scientists study the oceans?

_____

Name: _____   Date: _____

Directions: Over seventy-one percent of Earth is covered in water. The graph shows the sizes of different oceans and seas. Use the graph answer the questions.

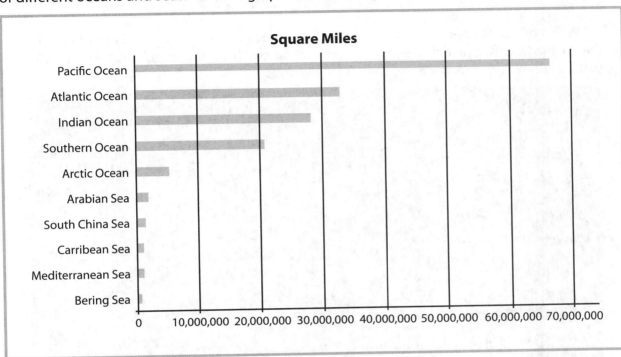

1. Which is the biggest ocean?

   a. Arctic

   c. Pacific

   b. Atlantic

   d. Indian

2. Which are the two smallest seas.

   a. Arabian Sea and
   South China Sea

   c. Bering Sea and
   Mediterranean Sea

   b. Mediterranean Sea and
   South China Sea

   d. Bering Sea and
   Arabian Sea

3. How much of Earth's surface is covered in water?

   _____

   _____

Analyzing Data

Name: _____ Date: _____

Directions: Read the text, and study the picture fo the Great Barrier Reef, and answer the questions.

While on vacation in Australia, Ella had the chance to visit the Great Barrier Reef in the Pacific Ocean. She could see it from the shore and from the boat. It is over 217,000 square kilometers and, it can be seen from the moon.

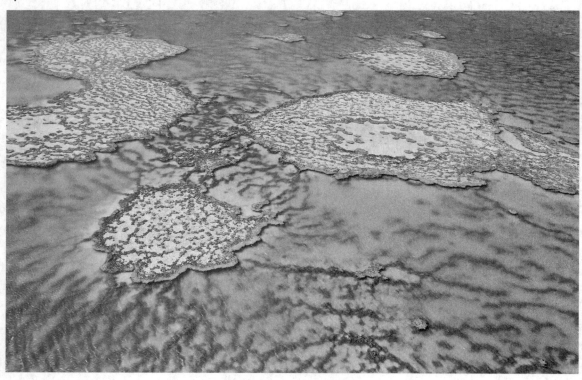

1. What ocean is the Great Barrier Reef located in?

   a. Atlantic   **b.** Indian

   c. Pacific   **d.** Arctic

2. How big is the Great Barrier Reef?

   a. 17,000 square kilometers   **b.** 217,000 square kilometers

   c. 217 square kilometers   **d.** 21 square kilometers

3. What question could you ask about the Pacific Ocean given the size of the Great Barrier Reef?

   _____

   _____

Name: _____ **Date:** _____

Directions: Label the map with the oceans of the world. Then, answer the question.

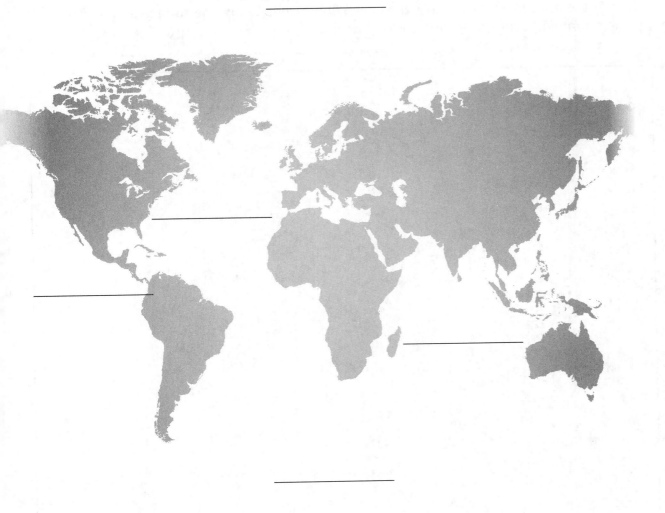

Planning Solutions

1. How could you learn more about the world's oceans?

_____

_____

_____

_____

Name: _____ **Date:** _____

Directions: Read the text, and draw a picture to show what you think the ocean floor looks like.

> At the bottom of the ocean is the ocean floor. Deep below the surface of the water are mountains, plains, volcanoes, and trenches.

Communicating Results

Name: _____ **Date:** _____

Directions: Read the text, and answer the questions.

Climate Change

Weather is local and short-term. It refers to atmospheric conditions over several minutes, and up to several days. Weather includes temperature, humidity, rain, snow, wind speeds, and wind direction. When we ask about the weather, we usually want to know about the weather where we live.

Climate is regional, global, and long-term. It refers to the averages of weather patterns, over seasons, years, or decades. The concept of climate is much bigger and broader than weather.

Climate change is a long-term change in Earth's climate, especially a change due to an increase in the average atmospheric temperature. Our planet is getting hotter. Glaciers are melting and our droughts are more severe. When public speakers and scientists talk about climate change, they usually mean "human-caused" changes. There has been a rapid increase of carbon dioxide and other greenhouse gases in the atmosphere. This is due to the burning of coal, oil, and gas.

Greenhouse gases are compared to a blanket that traps the sun's warmth near Earth's surface. This makes our planet hotter. Scientists say that there will be serious effects in the future from greenhouse gas emissions from cars and power plants.

Although plants and the ocean absorb carbon dioxide, they can't keep up with the extra amount that people have been releasing. Greenhouse gases stay in the atmosphere for a long time.

---

1. _____ refers to the state of the atmosphere over several minutes and up to several days.

   a. climate

   b. weather

   c. precipitation

   d. none of the above

2. _____ refers to the long-term average of weather, measured usually in decades.

   a. snow

   b. rain

   c. weather

   d. climate

3. What are some ways we can reduce the amount of carbon dioxide we produce?

   _____

   _____

Analyzing Data

Name: _____ Date: _____

Directions: Study the diagrams, and answer the questions.

Natural Greenhouse Effect   **Human-Enhanced Greenhouse Effect**

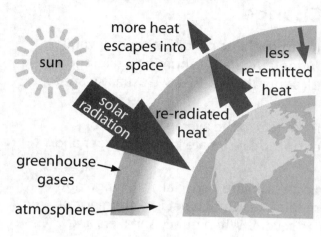 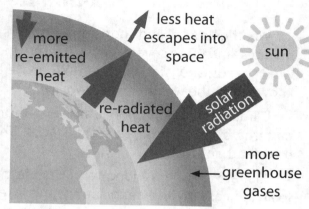

1. What is the same in both diagrams?

    a. the amount of re-emitted heat

    b. the amount of heat that escapes

    c. the amount of solar radiation

    d. the amount of greenhouse gases

2. What two things are different between the natural and human-enhanced greenhouse effects?

    a. amount of heat escaping and amount of heat re-emitted

    b. solar radiation

    c. sun

    d. nothing is different

3. Why are scientists concerned about climate change?

    _____

    _____

    _____

    _____

Name: _____ Date: _____

Directions: Read the text, and answer the questions.

Abby is at the Science Museum with her family. They are watching a presentation about the history transportation. One of Abby's sisters asks if cars cause pollution. The presenter tells them that up until 150 years ago human activity did not produce nearly as much greenhouse gases. The invention of the car and the use of fossil fuels release carbon dioxide and other greenhouse gases into the atmosphere.

1. What happened about 150 years ago, that created more greenhouse gases?

   a. election season

   b. war

   c. invention of cars

   d. a hurricane

2. What is the main greenhouse gas?

   a. butane

   b. carbon dioxide

   c. oxygen

   d. hydrogen

3. What question could you ask about the future of the planet, due to climate change and the use of fossil fuels?

_____

_____

_____

Planning Solutions

Name: _____   **Date:** _____

Directions: Read the text, and answer the questions.

> Simon lives in California. He and his friends are very careful when they go camping to put out any fires they have at night. They have a bucket of water near the campfire since the rest of the ground is so dry. Simon and his friends learned from the park rangers that climate change has caused an increase in wildfires.

1. Which climate change effect did Simon and his friends learn about?

   a. wildfires

   b. rising sea levels

   c. threats to animals and habitat

   d. mud slides

2. Why has their been an increase in wildfires?

   a. kids playing with matches

   b. too much rain

   c. climate change

   d. none of the above

3. What are the other the impacts of climate change?

   _____

   _____

51412—180 Days of Science

Name: _____ Date: _____

Directions: Use the word bank to complete the sentences.

carbon dioxide	heat waves	weather
climate	hotter	wildfires
climate change	human activity	

1. The most common type of greenhouse gas is _____ .

2. Long periods of time with above-normal temperatures are called _____ .

3. When _____ are not controlled, they can be deadly.

4. Scientific evidence paints a clear picture that _____ is happening.

5. Abuut 150 years ago, _____ started creating much more greenhouse gases.

6. _____ is local and short-term. It refers to atmospheric conditions over several minutes and up to several days.

7. _____ is regional, global, and long-term.

8. Our planet is getting _____ .

ABC

Communicating Results

Name: _____ **Date:** _____

Directions: Read the text, and answer the questions.

Taking Care of Our Environment

We know that climate change can increase wildfires, tornadoes, hurricanes, and drought. What might it be doing to our animal population?

Calculating extinction rates of animal species is not easy. That's because no one knows exactly how many species there are. Scientists have identified at least 1.9 million animal species. There are possibly many more that scientists have not yet discovered. Scientists agree that our animal populations are decreasing.

When too many species die out too quickly, the biodiversity of our planet suffers. Plants and animals need each other for maintaining the delicate balance of a healthy ecosystem for all living organisms.

1. How many species of animals have scientists identified?

   a. 5.3 million

   b. 2.1 thousand

   c. 1.9 million

   d. 19 thousand

2. When too many animal species die out too quickly, the _____ of our planet suffers.

   a. biodiversity

   b. axis

   c. rotation

   d. none of the above

3. Why do you think the rate of extinction is increasing?

   _____

   _____

   _____

   _____

Learning Content

Name: _____   **Date:** _____

Directions: Read the text, and answer the questions.

Mammals

Species	Location	Reason for Decline
bat	Indiana East & Midwest	habitat destruction
deer, key	South Florida	habitat destruction, road kills
elephant, Asian	South central & SE Asia	poisoning of food sources
gibbons	China, India, SE Asia	habitat destruction
mouse, salt march	California	habitat destruction
panda, giant	China	restricted habitat
prairie dog	West US	habitat destruction, poisoning
rhino, black	South Sahara in Africa	poaching for horn
rhino, white	Central and East Africa	poaching for horn
tiger	Temperate, tropical Asia	habitat destruction, sport hunting
wolf, red	Southeastern U.S. to Texas	habitat destruction, hunting, trapping, poisoning

 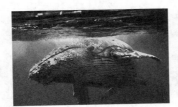 

1. The reason for the decline in the numbers of giant pandas is _____ .

   a. restricted habitat

   b. commercial hunting

   c. poaching

   d. road kills

2. What animal's numbers have declined in South Florida?

   a. prairie dog

   b. rhino

   c. key deer

   d. tiger

3. Which of the animal species mentioned above are you most concerned about? Why?

   _____

   _____

Name: _____   **Date:** _____

Developing Questions

Directions: Read the text, and answer the questions.

Peter visited the zoo on Saturday with his family. They spent most of their time in the monkey house. Peter loves gorillas and orangutans. He read on the exhibit wall that all gorillas are endangered. There are only 220,000 left in the wild and the females only give birth once every four years. That made Peter sad. Especially when he learned his other favorite animal the orangutan is also endangered. The handler said there were less than 60,000 left in the wild.

1. Female gorillas give birth every _____ years.

   a. two

   b. three

   c. four

   d. five

2. Approximately how many orangutans are left in the wild?

   a. 1,500

   b. 200

   c. 60,000

   d. 4,000

3. What question do you have about animal extinction?

   _____

   _____

Planning Solutions

Name: _____ **Date:** _____

Directions: Read the text, and answer the questions.

Ashley and her friends are in the supermarket looking for products that don't use animals for testing and use recycled materials.

They read the bottles of all the beauty products they plan to buy. Ashley finds two great products for her hair that don't test on animals and use recycled bottles. She knows companies that use recycled bottles produce less waste. That is good for the environment, especially for the animals

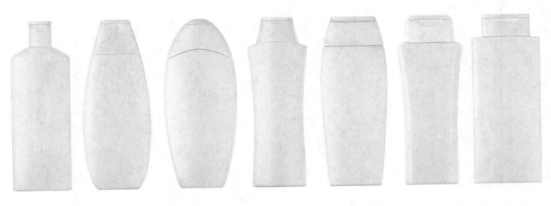

1. What are the two things that are important to Ashley and her friends about the products they are buying?

   a. cheap and colorful bottle

   b. desinger name and fragance

   c. not tested on animals and made from recycled materials.

   d. expensive and stylish

2. Why should we read labels?

   a. to avoid using products that have been tested on animals

   b. to see where the company headquarters is located

   c. to see if there are any calories in our shampoo

   d. none of the above

3. What could you do to learn more about using products that are good for the environment?

   _____

   _____

   _____

Name: _____ **Date:** _____

Directions: Pick one of the animals you learned about this week, and research ways they can be saved from extinction. Record your findings as a poster below.

Communicating Results

How We Can Help Save You

Name: _____   Date: _____

Directions: Read the text, and answer the questions.

Learning Content

Population and Resource Conservation

Almost everything we do involves our planet's natural resources. Every day, every moment, people all over Earth are using something from the natural world. We dig coal from underneath the ground. We drill into the surface of the Earth for oil and gas to power our cars and homes. We fish for food. We drink water.

Many of the things we do are damaging our Earth. Factories, power plants, and automobiles fill the air we breathe with dirty gases. Harmful chemicals damage our soils, and make our food unhealthy. Trees are cut to the ground in animal habitats.

Scientists tell us that we are using our natural resources so quickly that we will soon have critical shortages. This could cause conflict with other countries that need the same resources. It is a deeply complex problem that must be addressed.

1. What is one of the factors damaging our planet?

   a. clean air

   b. harmful chemicals

   c. trees

   d. clean water

2. Almost everything we do, every day, involves our planet's _____.

   a. orientation to the north

   b. relationship to other planets

   c. natural resources

   d. none of the above

3. Why should we care about our world's natural resources?

_____

_____

Analyzing Data

Name: _____ Date: _____

Directions: Read the text, study the chart, and answer the questions.

Studies show that the richest countries use about 10 times more of available resources than the poorest countries. Global use of materials is increasing. China's urban transformation requires huge amounts of iron, steel, cement, and energy.

Annual Material Used Per Person	
North America	34 tons
Asia	33 tons
South America	23 tons
Europe	20 tons
Africa	3 tons

1. Which continent uses the most material per person?

   a. North America

   b. Europe

   c. Africa

   d. Asia

2. Which continent uses the least material per person?

   a. Asia

   b. Africa

   c. North America

   d. Europe

3. If you were a scientist, how would you approach the problem of uneven distribution of the world's natural resources?

   _____

   _____

Name: _____ Date: _____

Directions: Read the text, and answer the questions.

Henri works overseas. He helps clean up the terrible living conditions in the world's poorest countries. He knows that global resources are not shared evenly. Many people in the world do not have safe drinking water. Polluted waters have brought disease to people who have the least.

Earth's Natural Resources

water	minerals	rivers	clay
air	iron	lakes	sand
coal	soil	mountains	copper
oil	forests & timber	farmlands	manganese
natural gas	rocks	wetlands	stone
phosphorus	sediments	coastal shores	

1. What vital natural resource is severely lacking in the poorest areas of the world?

   a. clean water

   b. new cellphones

   c. microwave ovens

   d. copper

2. Water, air, and food are essential to life. After looking at the list of Earth's natural resources, write a question about the one that seems most important to you.

   _____

   _____

   _____

3. Write a question to Henri.

   _____

   _____

   _____

Developing Questions

Planning Solutions

Directions: Read the text, and answer the questions.

"What can we do to keep our planet healthy?" is the name of the contest that Irondale Middle School is having. Barrett Roberts is the chairman. Every single class is participating. The class that shows that they have done the most in the next six months will win the grand prize. The winning class will take a whole day off from school to go to the State Fair.

Each class can choose activities from the list. All completed activities have to be recorded, signed, and dated by the teacher. The class that "does the most" wins.

- Plant vegetables.
- Plant fruit trees.
- Plant evergreen trees.
- Carpool every day.
- Recycle paper and glass bottles.
- Use energy-efficient LED light bulbs that last longer and are more durable.
- Print on both sides when making photocopies.
- Use cold water for washing clothes.
- Use an old-fashioned clothes line for drying clothes.
- Use only recycled paper.
- Make a compost pile.

1. What are three things that you would choose to do to win the contest?

_____

_____

_____

2. Why did you choose those three?

_____

_____

_____

_____

Name: _____ **Date:** _____

Directions: Put the steps of planting a tree in order. Then, ask an adult if you can plant a tree to help Earth.

- Decide what tree to plant.
- Enjoy your newly planted tree and know you helped Earth.
- Ask an adult where you can plant your tree.
- Dig the hole for the tree.
- Plant the tree and then give it some water.
- Ask an adult to take you to the local garden store to buy a small tree, or sapling.

Communicating Results

1. _____

2. _____

3. _____

4. _____

5. _____

6. _____

Answer Key

Life Science

Week 1: Day 1 (page 14)
1. a
2. b
3. All living things are made of cells. Cells are the basic units of life. Anything that is living is made of cells.

Week 1: Day 2 (page 15)
1. b
2. c
3. Plant cells contain a cell wall, look more rigid, and are rectangular in shape. Animal cells are less rigid and are round in shape. Vacuoles are small in animal cells. Plant cells contain chloroplast.

Week 1: Day 3 (page 16)
1. a
2. b
3. Questions will vary.

Week 1: Day 4 (page 17)
1. a
2. b
3. Animal cells are rounder in shape, while plants cells are more rectangular in shape.

Week 1: Day 5 (page 18)
1. animal cell
2. The cell is round in shape. There is no cell wall.

Week 2: Day 1 (page 19)
1. c
2. c
3. Animals don't need to convert light into sugar (energy). Animals eat food.

Week 2: Day 2 (page 20)
1. c
2. a
3. Plant and animal cells carry out similar functions. Cell membranes allow the flow of substances. Both have a nucleus to hold DNA. Both produce proteins. Both have vacuoles to store salts and sugars, though plant vacuoles are much larger.

Week 2: Day 3 (page 21)
1. b
2. a
3. Questions will vary.

Week 2: Day 4 (page 22)
1. d
2. a
3. The celery would turn red.

Week 2: Day 5 (page 23)
1. blue
2. yellow
3. purple

Week 3: Day 1 (page 24)
1. b
2. d
3. Plants release oxygen and water vapor through their leaves.

Week 3: Day 2 (page 25)
1. a
2. c
3. into the air

Week 3: Day 3 (page 26)
1. d
2. c
3. near a window so that the plant receives plenty of light

Week 3: Day 4 (page 27)
1. d
2. c
3. Investigations will vary.

Week 3: Day 5 (page 28)
Diagrams should look similar to the one depicted in Week 3, Day 2.

Week 4: Day 1 (page 29)
1. b
2. c
3. Nutrients, vitamins, minerals, and water are absorbed into the blood.

Week 4: Day 2 (page 30)
1. d
2. b
3. The esophagus squeezes food into the stomach.

Week 4: Day 3 (page 31)
1. b
2. c
3. Questions will vary.

Week 4: Day 4 (page 32)
1. Answers will vary. One way is to bring in a garden hose to show circumference, length, and coil.

Answer Key *(cont.)*

Week 4: Day 5 (page 33)
1. squeezes food into the stomach
2. where food is stored and wats to be processed
3. nutrients, vitamins, minerals, and water are absorbed into the blood

Week 5: Day 1 (page 34)
1. b
2. d

Week 5: Day 2 (page 35)
1. c
2. Answers will vary. Population ecology.

Week 5: Day 3 (page 36)
1. a
2. d
3. Questions will vary.

Week 5: Day 4 (page 37)
1. b
2. d
3. Answers will vary. He could test the amount of sunlight in the ecosystem. He could gauge the temperature of the ecosystem.

Week 5: Day 5 (page 38)
Diagrams will vary but should include all the elements asked for.

Week 6: Day 1 (page 39)
1. d
2. b

Week 6: Day 2 (page 40)
1. b
2. a
3. a

Week 6: Day 3 (page 41)
1. a
2. Questions will vary.
3. Questions will vary.
4. Questions will vary.

Week 6: Day 4 (page 42)
1. c
2. a
3. b
4. The results of his experimentations.

Week 6: Day 5 (page 43)
1. Plant reproduction
2. pollination
3. pollen
4. proboscis
5. Bees
6. red
7. wind

Week 7: Day 1 (page 44)
1. c
2. c
3. d

Week 7: Day 2 (page 45)
1. c
2. d

Week 7: Day 3 (page 46)
1. d
2. Questions will vary.
3. Questions will vary.
4. Questions will vary.

Week 7: Day 4 (page 47)
1. a
2. Plans will vary.
3. Plans will vary.

Week 7: Day 5 (page 48)
Charts will vary.

Week 8: Day 1 (page 49)
1. b
2. c
3. whether it's a whole-body fossil or a trace fossil

Week 8: Day 2 (page 50)
1. b
2. d

Week 8: Day 3 (page 51)
1. d
2. Questions will vary.
3. Questions will vary.

Week 8: Day 4 (page 52)
1. c
2. d
3. 1) An insect stepped in sticky tree resin many years ago; 2) The insect couldn't escape and eventually got covered in sticky resin; 3) After millions of years, the resin hardened into amber.

Answer Key *(cont.)*

Week 8: Day 5 (page 53)

2. It sinks to the ocean floor
3. soft parts rot away leaving behind the skeleton
6. water dissolves the rock leaving a skeleton-shaped hole
7. mineral-rich water fills the mold and it becomes a skeleton-shaped cast stone
8. the rock surrounding the fossil rises to Earth's surface

Week 9: Day 1 (page 54)

1. c
2. b
3. plenty of available sediment to cover and envelop dead organisms

Week 9: Day 2 (page 55)

1. d
2. d
3. Their bodies decompose.

Week 9: Day 3 (page 56)

1. c
2. Questions will vary.
3. Questions will vary.

Week 9: Day 4 (page 57)

1. d
2. b
3. Responses will vary.

Week 9: Day 5 (page 58)

The Tyrannosaurus Rex's size is bigger; body is bigger; back is longer and straighter; legs are longer and thicker; tail is longer and thicker; face is larger; it has hands whereas the horse doesn't.

Week 10: Day 1 (page 59)

1. a
2. b
3. Responses will vary.

Week 10: Day 2 (page 60)

1. d
2. b
3. d

Week 10: Day 3 (page 61)

1. b
2. c
3. Questions will vary.

Week 10: Day 4 (page 62)

star—gas
bicycle—wheel
tree—branch
clock—hands
Ferris wheel—seats
table—legs
chair—legs
mountain—rocks
blue jeans—pockets

Week 10: Day 5 (page 63)

1. Answers will vary.
2. Answers will vary.
3. Answers will vary.

Week 11: Day 1 (page 64)

1. b
2. c
3. Possible answer includes, "a change in environment/no food/weather change/adverse conditions."

Week 11: Day 2 (page 65)

1. b
2. c
3. Responses will vary.

Week 11: Day 3 (page 66)

1. d
2. d
3. Questions will vary.

Week 11: Day 4 (page 67)

1. d
2. c
3. Questions will vary.

Week 11: Day 5 (page 68)

migrate—to move from one type of place to another
permanent migration—to never return to the original home
seasonal migration—leaving in summer, and returning in winter
innate—inherited
trait—characteristic
imprinting—to identify with a certain species for life
learned behavior—acquired behavior

1. Responses will vary.

Week 12: Day 1 (page 69)

1. c
2. c
3. Answers will vary.

Answer Key *(cont.)*

Week 12: Day 2 (page 70)
1. c
2. c
3. Camels have thick eyelashes and have the ability to close their nostrils to keep sand out.

Week 12: Day 3 (page 71)
1. a
2. a
3. Questions will vary.

Week 12: Day 4 (page 72)
1. d
2. a

Week 12: Day 5 (page 73)
Responses will vary.

Physical Science

Week 1: Day 1 (page 74)
1. c
2. b
3. Responses will vary.

Week 1: Day 2 (page 75)
1. d
2. a
3. Responses will vary.

Week 1: Day 3 (page 76)
1. c
2. a
3. Questions will vary.

Week 1: Day 4 (page 77)
1. a
2. b
3. Responses will vary.

Week 1: Day 5 (page 78)
1. matter
2. atoms
3. protons, neutrons, electrons
4. hydrogen
5. 118
6. Any three of the following: oxygen, carbon, hydrogen, nitrogen, calcium, phosphorous

Week 2: Day 1 (page 79)
1. a
2. c
3. The form of the can has changed.

Week 2: Day 2 (page 80)
1. b
2. a
3. Responses will vary.

Week 2: Day 3 (page 81)
1. d
2. a
3. Questions will vary.

Week 2: Day 4 (page 82)
1. d
2. d
3. Responses will vary.

Week 2: Day 5 (page 83)
Crush a can.—physical
Change the shape of clay.—physical
Rip a piece of paper.—physical
Burn a piece of paper.—chemical
Get paper wet.—physical
Add Alka-Seltzer to water.—chemical
Melt ice.—physical
Burn fireworks.—chemical
Make bread from dough.—chemical
Add baking soda to vinegar.—chemical
Burn a candle.—chemical
Heat sugar to make caramel.—chemical

Week 3: Day 1 (page 84)
1. c
2. a
3. Because all products in our world are made from natural resources.

Week 3: Day 2 (page 85)
1. a
2. b
3. Questions will vary.

Week 3: Day 3 (page 86)
1. d
2. a
3. Questions will vary.

Week 3: Day 4 (page 87)
1. d
2. a
3. Responses will vary.

Answer Key (cont.)

Week 3: Day 5 (page 88)
1. tree
2. building
3. natural and synthetic
4. aspirin
5. resources
6. Vitamin D
7. Kevlar
8. sugar
9. paper, plastic
10. synthesis

Week 4: Day 1 (page 89)
1. c
2. b
3. Responses will vary.

Week 4: Day 2 (page 90)
1. a
2. b
3. because atoms that make up an object cannot be created or destroyed

Week 4: Day 3 (page 91)
1. b
2. b
3. Questions will vary.

Week 4: Day 4 (page 92)
1. a
2. d
3. Responses will vary.

Week 4: Day 5 (page 93)
1. Antoine Lavoisier
2. The Law of Conservation of Mass
3. products
4. atoms
5. sound
6. kinetic energy
7. mass
8. matter

Week 5: Day 1 (page 94)
1. c
2. b
3. Responses will vary.

Week 5: Day 2 (page 95)
1. c
2. b
3. Your body will continue to move forward.

Week 5: Day 3 (page 96)
1. b
2. c
3. Questions will vary.

Week 5: Day 4 (page 97)
1. d
2. a
3. Tests will vary.

Week 5: Day 5 (page 98)
Diagrams will vary.

Week 6: Day 1 (page 99)
1. b
2. c
3. Responses will vary.

Week 6: Day 2 (page 100)
1. c
2. d
3. Responses will vary.

Week 6: Day 3 (page 101)
1. a
2. b
3. Questions will vary.

Week 6: Day 4 (page 102)
1. a
2. c
3. Explanations will vary.

Week 6: Day 5 (page 103)
1. a
2. a
3. Responses will vary.

Week 7: Day 1 (page 104)
1. a
2. c
3. Responses will vary

Week 7: Day 2 (page 105)
1. b
2. c
3. Responses will vary.

Week 7: Day 3 (page 106)
1. c
2. a
3. Questions will vary.

Answer Key (cont.)

Week 7: Day 4 (page 107)
1. c
2. b
3. Responses will vary.

Week 7: Day 5 (page 108)
Explanations will vary.

Week 8: Day 1 (page 109)
1. b
2. a
3 Responses will vary.

Week 8: Day 2 (page 110)
1. b
2. a
3. midway

Week 8: Day 3 (page 111)
1. a
2. a
3. Questions will vary.

Week 8: Day 4 (page 112)
1. b
2. d
3. Responses will vary.

Week 8: Day 5 (page 113)
potential; kinetic
kinetic; potential
kinetic; potential
potential; kinetic
potential; kinetic

Week 9: Day 1 (page 114)
1. c
2. b
3. static electricity

Week 9: Day 2 (page 115)
1. c
2. a
3. any of the materials less likely to cause static electricity (wood, nickel, copper, silver)

Week 9: Day 3 (page 116)
1. b
2. c
3. Questions will vary.

Week 9: Day 4 (page 117)
1. b
2. a
3. Responses will vary.

Week 9: Day 5 (page 118)
fur; hands; leather jacket

Week 10: Day 1 (page 119)
1. d
2. d
3. Responses will vary.

Week 10: Day 2 (page 120)
1. b
2. c

Week 10: Day 3 (page 121)
1. b
2. b
3. Questions will vary.

Week 10: Day 4 (page 122)
1. b
2. there may not be wide access to electricity
3. Responses will vary.

Week 10: Day 5 (page 123)
1. hotter
2. metal
3. heat and light
4. heat transfer
5. sunlight

Week 11: Day 1 (page 124)
1. c
2. d
3. Sound travels faster through solids than liquids or air.

Week 11: Day 2 (page 125)
1. b
2. a
3. b

Week 11: Day 3 (page 126)
1. a
2. a
3. Questions will vary.

Answer Key *(cont.)*

Week 11: Day 4 (page 127)
1. a
2. Responses will vary.
3. Responses will vary. She can change the ingredient. She can change the intensity of the banging.

Week 11: Day 5 (page 128)
1. Yes. Responses will vary.

Week 12: Day 1 (page 129)
1. c
2. c
3. Responses will vary.

Week 12: Day 2 (page 130)
1. a
2. c

Week 12: Day 3 (page 131)
1. a
2. c
3. Questions will vary.

Week 12: Day 4 (page 132)
1. a
2. Models will vary.

Week 12: Day 5 (page 133)
1. black
2. opaque
3. transparent
4. translucent
5. reflected
6. crests
7. reflected
8. wave
9. wavelength
10. optics
11. green, absorbs

Earth and Space Science

Week 1: Day 1 (page 134)
1. b
2. c
3. Each phase of the moon is determined by how much of the moon we can see from Earth.

Week 1: Day 2 (page 135)
1. a
2. a
3. Drawings should show the moon partly in Earth's shadow.

Week 1: Day 3 (page 136)
1. b
2. She would see all phases of the moon.
3. Questions will vary.

Week 1: Day 4 (page 137)
1. b
2. The rays are less intense than summer and more intense than winter.
3. Roger can put his model on a device that allows it to tilt.

Week 1: Day 5 (page 138)
1. Drawings will vary.

Week 2: Day 1 (page 139)
1. a
2. b
3. Because Earth's gravitational pull is so strong, we don't notice the pull from other objects.

Week 2: Day 2 (page 140)
1. a
2. Responses will vary based on weight of child.

Week 2: Day 3 (page 141)
1. Answers should describe that the moon would continue in a straight path or that it may start orbiting another body.
2. mass
3. Questions will vary.
4. Questions will vary.

Week 2: Day 4 (page 142)
1. b
2. He would place the Milky Way outside the center of the solar system.
3. Responses will vary. The moon rotates around the earth. The earth rotates around the sun. The sun rotates around the center of the Milky Way Galaxy.

Week 2: Day 5 (page 143)
1. It would be much harder since you would weigh much more.

Week 3: Day 1 (page 144)
1. c
2. b
3. Responses will vary.

Week 3: Day 2 (page 145)
1. b
2. c
3. Neptune, since it is the farthest from the sun.

Answer Key *(cont.)*

Week 3: Day 3 (page 146)
1. c
2. b
3. Questions will vary.

Week 3: Day 4 (page 147)
1. b
2. c
3. She can use smaller objects to make the dwarf planets than the ones she uses to make the regular planets.

Week 3: Day 5 (page 148)
1. Responses may vary. Stars, moons, dust, and asteroids.

Week 4: Day 1 (page 149)
2. c
3. b
4. Responses will vary.

Week 4: Day 2 (page 150)
1. b
2. c
3. Responses will vary.

Week 4: Day 3 (page 151)
1. a
2. No because the first bird fossils were found around 201 million years ago.
3. Questions will vary.

Week 4: Day 4 (page 152)
1. d
2. d
3. Responses will vary.

Week 4: Day 5 (page 153)
1. Responses will vary. The oldest layer will always be on the bottom and the newest layer on the top.
2. Responses may include that older layers are beneath younger layers.

Week 5: Day 1 (page 154)
1. c
2. b
3. Weathering and erosion are similar but during weathering debris is not carried away.

Week 5: Day 2 (page 155)
1. a
2. b
3. Responses will vary.

Week 5: Day 3 (page 156)
1. c
2. Responses will vary.
3. Questions will vary.

Week 5: Day 4 (page 157)
1. b
2. c
3. Responses will vary.

Week 5: Day 5 (page 158)
1. Responses will vary.

Week 6: Day 1 (page 159)
1. c
2. b
3. Responses will vary.

Week 6: Day 2 (page 160)
1. a
2. b
3. Responses will vary

Week 6: Day 3 (page 161)
1. b
2. c
3. Questions will vary.

Week 6: Day 4 (page 162)
1. a
2. c
3. Responses will vary.

Week 6: Day 5 (page 163)
Students write a story about a dinosaur on Pangaea.

Week 7: Day 1 (page 164)
1. c
2. a
3. Everything would die out.

Week 7: Day 2 (page 165)
1. b
2. b
3. Eating a dead animal.

Week 7: Day 3 (page 166)
1. a
2. a
3. Questions will vary.

Week 7: Day 4 (page 167)
Plans will vary.

Answer Key *(cont.)*

Week 7: Day 5 (page 168)
Worm—decomposer
Peach tree—producer
Lion—consumer
Apple Tree—producer
Cabbage—producer
Robin—consumer
Catfish—consumer
Deer—consumer
Fungus—decomposer

Week 8: Day 1 (page 169)
1. c
2. b
3. Responses will vary.

Week 8: Day 2 (page 170)
1. a
2. d
3. Responses will vary.

Week 8: Day 3 (page 171)
1. b
2. c
3. a
4. Questions will vary.

Week 8: Day 4 (page 172)
1. Responses will vary.

Week 8: Day 5 (page 173)
1. Weathering
2. Erosion
3. Deposition

Week 9: Day 1 (page 174)
1. d
2. a
3. Responses will vary.

Week 9: Day 2 (page 175)
1. c
2. a
3. Over seventy-one percent

Week 9: Day 3 (page 176)
1. c
2. b
3. How big is the Pacific Ocean?

Week 9: Day 4 (page 177)
Arctic
Atlantic
Pacific
Indian
Antarctic
1. Responses will vary

Week 9: Day 5 (page 178)
Students draw a picture of the ocean floor.

Week 10: Day 1 (page 179)
1. b
2. d
3. Responses will vary.

Week 10: Day 2 (page 180)
1. c
2. a
3. Responses will vary.

Week 10: Day 3 (page 181)
1. c
2. b
3. Questions will vary.

Week 10: Day 4 (page 182)
1. a
2. c
3. Responses will vary.

Week 10: Day 5 (page 183)
1. carbon dioxide
2. heat waves
3. wildfires
4. climate change
5. Weather
6. Climate
7. hotter

Week 11: Day 1 (page 184)
1. c
2. a
3. Responses may vary.

Week 11: Day 2 (page 185)
1. a
2. c
3. Responses will vary.

Week 11: Day 3 (page 186)
1. c
2. c
3. Questions will vary.

Answer Key *(cont.)*

Week 11: Day 4 (page 187)
1. c
2. a
3. Responses will vary.

Week 11: Day 5 (page 188)
1. Students draw a picture of their favorite endangered animal.

Week 12: Day 1 (page 189)
1. b
2. c
3. Responses will vary.

Week 12: Day 2 (page 190)
1. a
2. b
3. Responses will vary.

Week 12: Day 3 (page 191)
1. a
2. Responses will vary.
3. Question will vary.

Week 12: Day 4 (page 192)
1. Responses will vary.
2. Responses will vary.

Week 12: Day 5 (page 193)
1. Ask an adult where you can plant your tree.
2. Decide what tree to plant.
3. Ask an adult to take you to the local garden store to buy a small tree, or sampling.
4. Dig the hole for your tree.
5. Plant the tree and give it some water.
6. Enjoy your newly planted tree and know you helped Earth.

Light Wave Diagram

Periodic Table

1	2	3	4	5	6	7	8	9	10	11	12	13	14	15	16	17	18
1 H 1.0079 Hydrogen																	**2** He 4.0026 Helium
3 Li 1.941 Lithium	**4** Be 9.0122 Beryllium											**5** B 10.811 Boron	**6** C 12.011 Carbon	**7** N 14.007 Nitrogen	**8** O 15.999 Oxygen	**9** F 18.998 Fluorine	**10** Ne 20.180 Neon
11 Na 22.990 Sodium	**12** Mg 24.305 Magnesium											**13** Al 26.982 Aluminium	**14** Si 28.086 Silicon	**15** P 30.974 Phosphorus	**16** S 32.065 Sulfur	**17** Cl 35.453 Chlorine	**18** Ar 39.948 Argon
19 K 39.098 Potassium	**20** Ca 40.078 Calcium	**21** Sc 44.956 Scandium	**22** Ti 47.867 Titanium	**23** V 50.942 Vanadium	**24** Cr 51.996 Chromium	**25** Mn 54.938 Manganese	**26** Fe 55.845 Iron	**27** Co 58.933 Cobalt	**28** Ni 58.693 Nickel	**29** Cu 63.546 Cooper	**30** Zn 65.39 Zinc	**31** Ga 69.723 Gallium	**32** Ge 1.0079 Germanium	**33** As 74.992 Arsenic	**34** Se 78.96 Selenium	**35** Br 79.904 Bromine	**36** Kr 83.80 Krypton
37 Rb 85.468 Rubidium	**38** Sr 87.62 Strontium	**39** Y 88.906 Yttrium	**40** Zr 91.224 Zirconium	**41** Nb 92.906 Niobium	**42** Mo 95.94 Molybdenum	**43** Tc 98 Technetium	**44** Ru 101.07 Ruthenium	**45** Rh 102.91 Rhodium	**46** Pd 106.42 Palladium	**47** Ag 107.87 Silver	**48** Cd 112.41 Cadmium	**49** In 114.82 Indium	**50** Sn 118.71 Tin	**51** Sb 121.76 Antimony	**52** Te 127.60 Tellurium	**53** I 126.90 Iodine	**54** Xe 131.29 Xenon
55 Cs 132.91 Cesium	**56** Ba 137.33 Barium	**57 - 71** La-Lu Lanthanide	**72** Hf 178.49 Hafnium	**73** Ta 180.95 Tantalum	**74** W 183.84 Tungsten	**75** Re 186.21 Rhenium	**76** Os 190.23 Osmium	**77** Ir 192.22 Iridium	**78** Pt 195.08 Platinum	**79** Au 196.97 Gold	**80** Hg 200.59 Mercury	**81** Tl 204.38 Thallium	**82** Pb 207.2 Lead	**83** Bi 208.98 Bismuth	**84** Po 209 Polonium	**85** At 210 Astatine	**86** Rn 222 Radon
87 Fr 223 Francium	**88** Ra 226 Radium	**89 - 103** Ac-Lr Actinide	**104** Rf 261 Rutherfordium	**105** Db 262 Dubnium	**106** Sg 266 Seaborgium	**107** Bh 264 Bohrium	**108** Hs 269 Hassium	**109** Mt 268 Meitnerium	**110** Ds Darmstadtium	**111** Rg 280 Roentgenium	**112** Cn 285 Copernicium	**113** Nh 286 Nihonium	**114** Fl 289 Flerovium	**115** Mc 293 Moscovium	**116** Lv 293 Livermorium	**117** Ts 294 Tennessine	**118** Og 294 Oganesson

Lanthanide series

57 La 138.91 Lanthanide	**58** Ce 140.12 Cerium	**59** Pr 140.91 Praseodymium	**60** Nd 144.24 Neodymium	**61** Pm 145 Promethium	**62** Sm 150.36 Samarium	**63** Eu 151.96 Europium	**64** Gd 157.25 Gadolinium	**65** Tb 158.93 Terbium	**66** Dy 162.5 Dysprosium	**67** Ho 164.93 Holmium	**68** Er 1.0079 Erbium	**69** Tm 168.93 Thulium	**70** Yb 173.04 Ytterbium	**71** Lu 1.0079 Lutetium

Actinide series

89 Ac 227 Actinide	**90** Th 232.04 Thorium	**91** Pa 231.04 Protactinium	**92** U 238.03 Uranium	**93** Np 237 Neptunium	**94** Pu 244 Plutonium	**95** Am 243 Americium	**96** Cm 247 Curium	**97** Bk 247 Berkelium	**98** Cf 251 Californium	**99** Es 252 Einsteinium	**100** Fm 257 Fermium	**101** Md 258 Mendelevium	**102** No 259 Nobelium	**103** Lr 1.0079 Lawrencium

Phases of the Moon

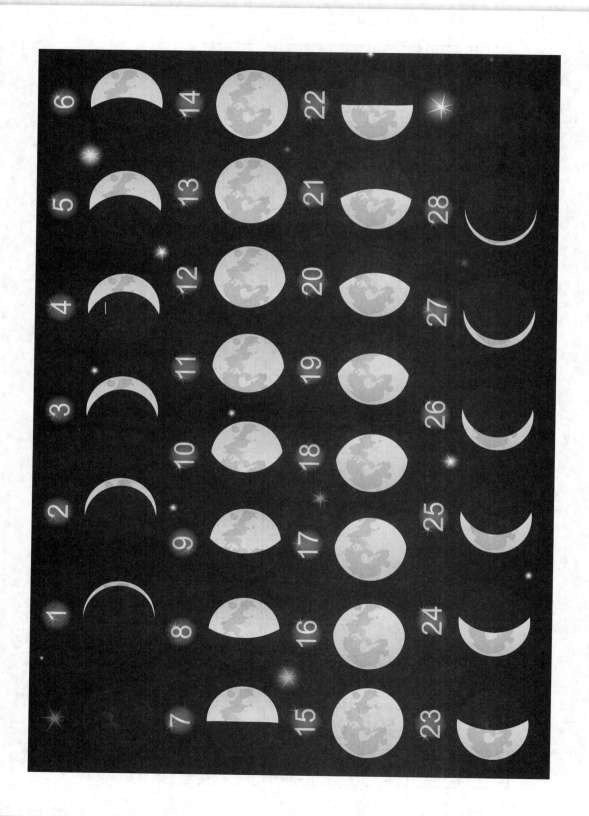

51412—180 Days of Science

© Shell Education

The Carbon Cycle

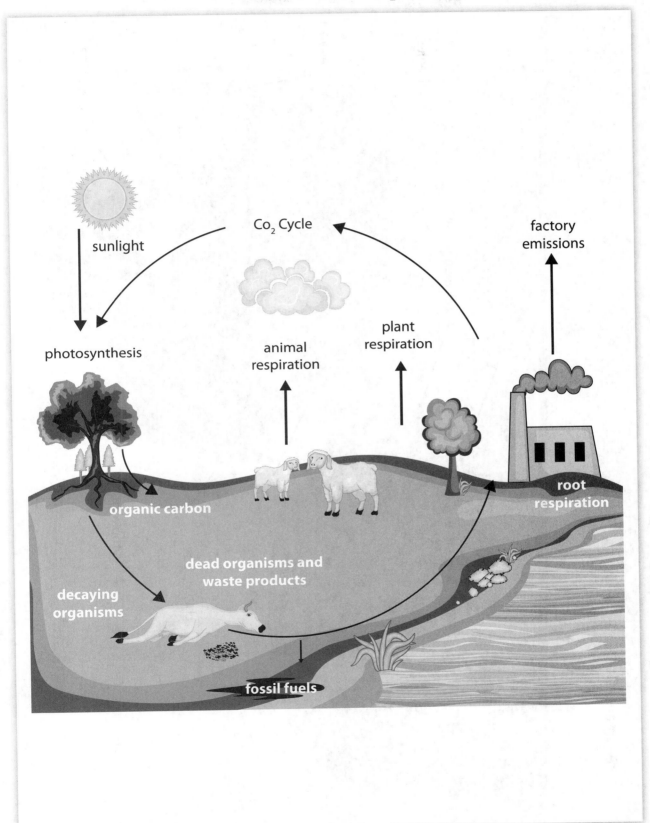

Plant and Animal Cells

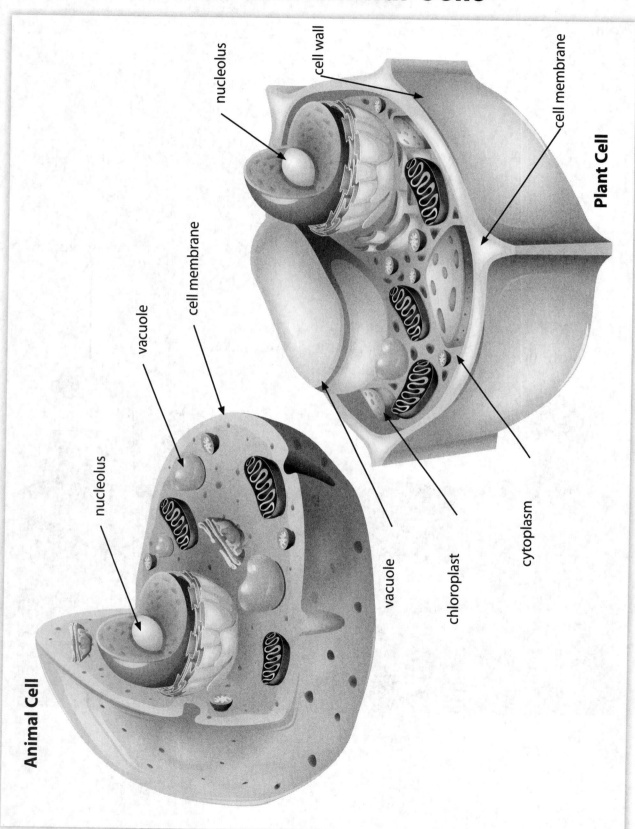

nucleolus

cell wall

cell membrane

Plant Cell

cell membrane

vacuole

nucleolus

vacuole

chloroplast

cytoplasm

Animal Cell

Notes

Developing Questions Rubric

Directions: Complete this rubric every four weeks to evaluate students' Day 3 activity sheets. Only one rubric is needed per student. Their work over the four weeks can be evaluated together. Evaluate their work in each category by writing a score in each row. Then, add up their scores, and write the total on the line. Students may earn up to 5 points in each row and up to 15 points total.

Skill	5	3	1	Score
Forming Scientific Inquiries	Forms scientific inquiries related to text all or nearly all the time.	Forms scientific inquiries related to text most of the time.	Does not form scientific inquiries related to text.	
Interpreting Text	Correctly interprets texts to answer questions all or nearly all the time.	Correctly interprets texts to answer questions most of the time.	Does not correctly interpret texts to answer questions.	
Applying Information	Applies new information to form scientific questions all or nearly all the time.	Applies new information to form scientific questions most of the time.	Does not apply new information to form scientific questions.	

Total Points: _____

Planning Solutions Rubric

Directions: Complete this rubric every four weeks to evaluate students' Day 4 activity sheets. Only one rubric is needed per student. Their work over the four weeks can be evaluated together. Evaluate their work in each category by writing a score in each row. Then, add up their scores, and write the total on the line. Students may earn up to 5 points in each row and up to 15 points total.

Skill	5	3	1	Score
Planning Investigations	Plans reasonable investigations to study topics all or nearly all the time.	Plans reasonable investigations to study topics most of the time.	Does not plan reasonable investigations to study topics.	
Making Predictions	Studies events to make reasonable predictions all or nearly all the time.	Studies events to make reasonable predictions most of the time.	Does not study events to make reasonable predictions.	
Choosing Next Steps	Chooses reasonable next steps for investigations all or nearly all the time.	Chooses reasonable next steps for investigations most of the time.	Does not choose reasonable next steps for investigations.	

Total Points: _____

Student Name: _____ **Date:** _____

Communicating Results Rubric

Directions: Complete this rubric every four weeks to evaluate students' Day 5 activity sheets. Only one rubric is needed per student. Their work over the four weeks can be evaluated together. Evaluate their work in each category by writing a score in each row. Then, add up their scores, and write the total on the line. Students may earn up to 5 points in each row and up to 15 points total.

Skill	5	3	1	Score
Representing Data	Correctly represents data with charts and graphs all or nearly all the time.	Correctly represents data with charts and graphs most of the time.	Does not correctly represents data with charts and graphs.	
Making Connections	Makes reasonable connections between new information and prior knowledge all or nearly all the time.	Makes reasonable connections between new information and prior knowledge most of the time.	Does not make reasonable connections between new information and prior knowledge.	
Explaining Results	Uses evidence to accurately explain results all or nearly all the time.	Uses evidence to accurately explain results most of the time.	Does not use evidence to accurately explain results.	

Total Points: _____

Life Science Analysis Chart

Directions: Record the total of each student's Day 1 and Day 2 scores from the four weeks. Then, record each student's rubric scores (pages 210–212). Add the totals, and record the sums in the Total Scores column. Record the average class score in the last row.

Student Name	Week 4						Week 8						Week 12						Total Scores
	Day 1	Day 2	DQ	PS	CR		Day 1	Day 2	DQ	PS	CR		Day 1	Day 2	DQ	PS	CR		
Average Classroom Score																			

DQ = Developing Questions, PS = Planning Solutions, CR = Communicating Results

Physical Science Analysis Chart

Directions: Record the total of each student's Day 1 and Day 2 scores from the four weeks. Then, record each student's rubric scores (pages 210–212). Add the totals, and record the sums in the Total Scores column. Record the average class score in the last row.

Student Name	Week 4						Week 8						Week 12						Total Scores
	Day 1	Day 2	DQ	PS	CR		Day 1	Day 2	DQ	PS	CR		Day 1	Day 2	DQ	PS	CR		
Average Classroom Score																			

DQ = Developing Questions, PS = Planning Solutions, CR = Communicating Results

Earth and Space Science Analysis Chart

Directions: Record the total of each student's Day 1 and Day 2 scores from the four weeks. Then, record each student's rubric scores (pages 210–212). Add the totals, and record the sums in the Total Scores column. Record the average class score in the last row.

Student Name	Week 4						Week 8						Week 12						Total Scores
	Day 1	Day 2	DQ	PS	CR		Day 1	Day 2	DQ	PS	CR		Day 1	Day 2	DQ	PS	CR		
Average Classroom Score																			

DQ = Developing Questions, PS = Planning Solutions, CR = Communicating Results

Digital Resources

To access digital resources, go to this website and enter the following code: 31939921
www.teachercreatedmaterials.com/administrators/download-files/

Rubrics

Resource	Filename
Developing Questions Rubric	questionsrubric.pdf
Planning Solutions Rubric	solutionsrubric.pdf
Communicating Results Rubric	resultsrubric.pdf

Item Analysis Sheets

Resource	Filename
Life Science Analysis Chart	LSanalysischart.pdf
	LSanalysischart.docx
	LSanalysischart.xlsx
Physical Science Analysis Chart	PSanalysischart.pdf
	PSanalysischart.docx
	PSanalysischart.xlsx
Earth and Space Science Analysis Chart	ESSanalysischart.pdf
	ESSanalysischart.docx
	ESSanalysischart.xlsx

Standards

Resource	Filename
Standards Charts	standards.pdf